HOLIDAYS
ON PARADE

24 Wall Quilts To Celebrate Special Occasions

Marie Shirer & Marla Stefanelli

Leman
Quilt Books

Introduction

Holidays are times to celebrate with good cheer, family and friends all pieced together in a merry quilt of fun. What better way to add to the festivities than by making, displaying and giving merry little quilts to honor the occasion?

That's what this book is all about: wall quilts to celebrate holidays and other special occasions. It is a book that came into being almost seamlessly as a sequel to *Christmas On Parade: 18 fast & easy wall quilts to celebrate the season.* We had so much fun designing, sewing and writing for that book that we didn't want the party to end. Plus our colleagues and readers wanted more. So we named all our favorite holidays and family events and came up with 24 new quilts for this book. All of the quilts are just right for the wall, but two of them are also big enough for baby quilts. And many of the holidays have more than one design that can be easily combined to make a larger quilt or to hang as a grouping. Check out the Thanksgiving trio to see what we mean.

Although each quilt in the book was inspired by a holiday or other occasion, most of them can be enjoyed year 'round. Certainly Raggedy Ann and Raggedy Andy will light up a room with their endearing smiles and crimson hair, whether they are delivering valentine greetings or not. Our Leprechaun can be your mascot even if you aren't a descendant of St. Patrick himself. The May Basket is a pretty basket of flowers that is never out of season. And Mom and Dad will love their quilts long after their special days have been celebrated. Our cat quilts come in two sizes. The smaller one has a patriotic flair, while the larger one simply celebrates cats with personality galore. Because for a clever cat, every day is a holiday.

Some of the quilts are especially suited to personalizing. Mark your children's accomplishments by embroidering their names, grades and schools on the School Days quilts. Celebrate a new baby with Bring in the New. Treat lovesick newlyweds to a light-hearted wedding keepsake with Cupid's Arrow.

We hope you enjoy making and giving these quilts as much as we have. Let the celebration begin!

Marie and Marla

Contents

Special Techniques

The quilts in this book have been designed to use several special techniques that are not only easy and quick, but a lot of fun as well. These special methods are explained here, at the beginning of the book, so you can read about them before starting your projects. However, at the back of the book, on pages 73-78, you will also find General Instructions for all the basic techniques used to make these quilts. The information covered there includes sizing, selecting fabrics, cutting patches, piecing, appliqué, embroidery, adding borders and corner squares, assembling the layers and quilting, adding tabs or a sleeve, binding the quilt and making a label. If you are a beginning quilter, be sure to read that section (as well as this one) to find a lot of helpful instruction. If you have made quilts before, you might want to use that section mainly for reference when questions arise.

3-D Piecing

This technique gives extra dimension for areas such as hair bangs on the Pilgrim Girl, ears (Easter Bunny, School Kids), the brim on Uncle Sam's hat, the handle on the May Basket, and Santa's mittens. Patches that are 3-D pieced have a double layer of fabric, except for Raggedy Ann's and Andy's hair, which are made with raw-edged strips of fabric.

Each set of project directions will tell you which patches to use for 3-D piecing and how to sew them. Patches are cut and folded with wrong sides together or are sewn before being basted to other patches. For example, the Pilgrim Boy has triangles of hair that are 3-D pieced over a square face.

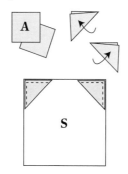

Simply follow the directions to add the 3-D patches before piecing the quilt top. The basted edges will be caught in the seams.

For the Pilgrim Girl and the School Girl, the hair bangs are cut from a rectangle of fabric that is folded in half lengthwise. Project directions will show you how to place the folded fabric to create the desired angle. After basting, trim the edges of the folded strip so that the hair patch matches the shape of the face.

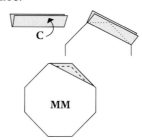

Some patches will need to be sewn to make the 3-D patch. The Easter Bunny's ears and Santa's mittens are done this way. Just follow project patterns and directions to sew these pieces right sides together. Turn them right side out, press and baste them in place before piecing the quilt top.

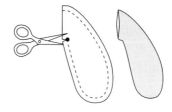

3-D Appliqué

This technique is similar to 3-D piecing, except that appliqués are made with a double layer of fabric and are sewn to the quilt after it is quilted and bound. Examples of projects where 3-D appliqué can be used include the stars on Old Glory and the hearts on Cupid's Arrow. All patches that can be done in 3-D appliqué can also be made with traditional hand appliqué if you prefer.

To make 3-D appliqués, cut patches that include ¼" seam allowances. Sew two patches with right sides together. Turning small patches right side out will be hard on the patch, so use a short stitch to make strong seams. Or you can sew the seam twice.

Clip inner curves or indentations of seams and trim seam allowances on points. Trim one seam allowance to be ⅛" wide and trim the other to be either a little wider or narrower.

Cut a small slit (about 1" long) in the patch that will be the back side. Cut carefully to be sure only one layer of fabric is slit. Turn appliqué right side out through the slit. Use a pin or needle to gently pull the seam to form a smooth edge; press flat.

3-D appliqués are sewn in place after the quilting and binding are finished. To attach 3-D appliqués, pin them in place with the slit side touching the quilt. Working from the back side of the quilt, take a few hand stitches through all layers of the quilt to hold the appliqué in place.

Some 3-D appliqués, such as the stars on Old Glory, will be sewn in place with a button on top. It's a good idea to use thread that matches the appliqué or button (not the quilt lining) so stitches will not be noticeable on the front of the quilt.

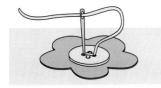

Some flowers can be attached by machine quilting around the flower centers through all layers.

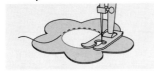

Embellishments

There are no limits to the kind and amount of embellishments you can use on these quilts. Feel free to use any or all of the options given here and in the project directions, but also add other objects, trims and techniques as you wish.

Embellishments fall into two categories: those that are added as the quilt top is made and before it is quilted, and those that are added after the quilting and binding are finished. The difference is that the first category has techniques and items that are flat and therefore will not interfere with the quilting. The second category has techniques and objects that are bulkier and therefore could interfere with the quilting.

Those Added Before Quilting

Adding Flat Trims: Ribbon, lace and braid are all good choices for embellishing these quilts. Project directions will explain where trims go and when to add them. In general, you want to baste or appliqué the trim to the fabric patch before piecing the patches so the ends will be caught in seams.

Use thread to match the trim, not the background. Trims also can be machine appliquéd with invisible nylon sewing thread and blind stitch. Ribbon should be sewn on both edges (not down the middle) so it doesn't curl up.

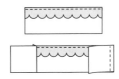

Those Added After Quilting

Embellishments that are added after quilting are usually sewn through all layers of the quilt. Select thread to match the embellishment, except for buttons if you want a contrasting thread.

Buttons: Choose buttons that have holes through the button itself or select buttons with a short shank.

Beads, Ribbon Bows and Other Doodads: These are sewn in place according to their type and location. For example, the School Girl can get her ears "pierced" by sewing a single gold bead to each earlobe. Or, if you prefer, use real dangling earrings that are just poked through the girl's ears. Speaking of jewelry, Mom's pearls are made simply by sewing a length of strong thread through the quilt from the back, stringing beads, fastening the end and couching the necklace in a couple of places.

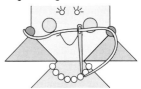

Once you begin thinking about embellishments, many other ideas will surely occur to you. The important thing is to have a lot of fun.

Bring in the New

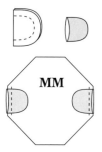

Color photo is on page 37.

Whether you are celebrating a new year or a new baby, this quilt will fill the bill. When choosing fabrics, remember the simple rule: light colors appear closer than dark colors. So for the banner, select a light shade for the patch with the letters to bring it forward.

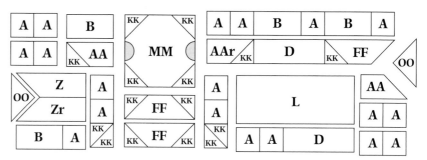

Piecing Diagram

▢ = 3-D piecing or appliqué

Assembly

1 Lay out all patches as shown in the piecing diagram.

2 To make ears, sew two ear patches (with right sides together) along curved edge. Turn right side out and press flat. Repeat for other ear. Baste ears to opposite sides of MM patch as shown here.

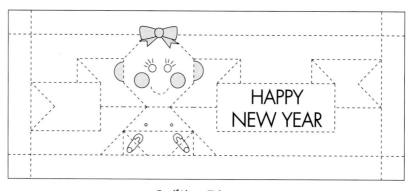

3 See next page for hints about tracing lettering or adding a baby's name and date.

Center L (banner) patch over "Happy New Year" lettering. Use red Micron Pigma pen to trace letters and fill them in.

4 Join lettered patches as shown in the piecing diagram. Wherever possible, press seam allowances toward the baby or banner. If necessary, trim dark seam allowances to prevent them from showing through lighter fabric.

5 Appliqué cheeks. Use two ply floss for all embroidery. With red floss and outline stitch, embroider mouth. Using blue floss and straight stitches, embroider eyelashes. With peach floss and single french knots, make two nipples.

6 Referring to the general instructions, add border strips and corner squares. Press seam allowances toward the

borders.

7 Referring to the general instructions, assemble lining, batting and quilt top. Quilt in-the-ditch as shown in the quilting diagram. Bind the quilt. Add tabs or sleeve if desired; see page 77 for information.

8 Add button eyes. Tie ribbon in a bow and tack to top of head. Insert safety pins in diaper.

Quilting Diagram

Cutting Requirements

Finished size: 26¼" x 11¼"

Ydg.	Fabric	Use	Cut
⅛ yd.	Purple Print	borders	2 K, 2 F
¼ yd.	Yellow Stripe	binding, border corners, banner	1½" x 83", 4 A, 1 Z, 1 Zr, 1 L
⅛ yd.	Blue Print	background	8 A, 4 B, 6 KK, 2 D, 2 OO
⅛ yd.	Purple/Red Print	background	9 A
¼ yd.	Peach Mini Check	face, ears, body	1 MM, 4 ear patches, 1 FF, 2 KK
⅛ yd.*	Pink Print	cheeks	2 cheeks
⅛ yd.	Yellow Print	banner	2 AA, 1 AAr, 1 FF, 2 A, 2 KK
⅛ yd.*	Peach Print	banner	3 KK
⅛ yd.*	Cream Print	diaper	1 FF
⅛ yd.*	White Print	diaper	2 KK
½ yd.	Light Solid	lining	30" x 15"

*only a very small amount is needed: see pattern(s) for size

Also Needed: 2 ¼" blue buttons for eyes, blue embroidery floss for eyelashes, red embroidery floss for mouth, peach embroidery floss for nipples, 15" of ¾"-wide pink ribbon for bow, 2 1" safety pins for diaper, red Micron Pigma pen for tracing letters, 30" x 15" batting

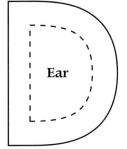

Ear

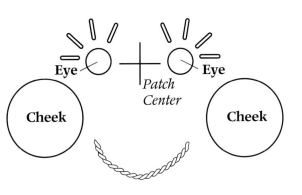

Eye · Patch Center · Eye

Cheek · Cheek

Add ³⁄₁₆" turn-under allowance to all appliqué patches.

Hints About Inked Lettering

1 If you can't easily see the lettering through the fabric, work on a glass table or window with light shining from behind the lettering.

2 Tape the pattern in place and hold or tape the fabric securely to keep it from shifting while you work.

3 For a baby announcement, find letters and numbers on page 48. Trace them on tracing paper, working one line at a time. Then cut out the lines of "type" and center them in the arrangement you like. Photocopy the final lettering (enlarging or reducing it to fit the L patch) and trace on fabric.

> Happy Baby
> Born July 15, 1996
> 7 lbs. 4 oz.

HAPPY NEW YEAR

Color photo is on page 38.

Cupid's Arrow

Will Cupid's arrow hit its mark? Sure, he is a little bit silly, but love is often like that. For a fun wedding or anniversary gift, embroider the names of the happy couple and the date of celebration below the large pieced heart.

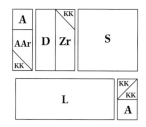

Piecing Diagram

Assembly

1 Lay out all patches as shown in the piecing diagram.

2 Join lettered patches as shown in the piecing diagram. Wherever possible, press seam allowances toward the cupid. If necessary, trim dark seam allowances to prevent them from showing through light fabric.

3 Referring to the general instructions, add border strips and corner squares. Press seam allowances toward the borders.

4 Appliqué wing, opening the seam to tuck in the lower straight edge. Close seam. Appliqué the large hearts, archer's bow and hair.

5 Use two ply of floss for all embroidery. Using gold floss and referring to illustration on next page, embroider arrow with chain stitch. With red floss, embroider bow string and mouth with outline stitch. Using black floss, embroider eyebrows with single straight stitches. Appliqué arrow point at top of arrow.

6 Referring to the general instructions, assemble lining, batting and quilt top. Quilt in-the-ditch as shown in the quilting diagram. Bind the quilt. Add tabs or sleeve if desired; see page 77 for information.

7 Tie ribbon to make bow tie. Sew bow tie to quilt at neck. For 3-D hearts, place two small heart patches right sides together and sew around the edge. Carefully cut a small slit in one layer, and turn the heart through the slit. Press flat. Repeat for second heart. Sew each heart to quilt (with slit side touching quilt), stitching through a pink or red button and all layers.

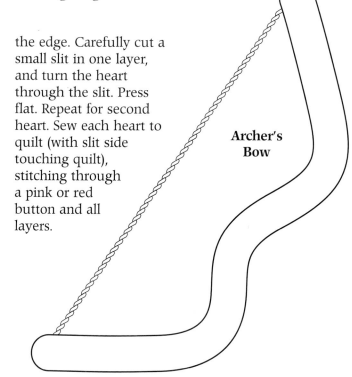

Archer's Bow

Quilting Diagram

Cutting Requirements

Finished size: 26¼" x 11¼"

Ydg.	Fabric	Use	Cut
⅛ yd.	Blue Print	borders, shorts	2 K, 2 F, 1 A, 1 GG
¼ yd.	Red Print	binding, border corners, hearts	1½" x 83", 4 A, 1 AAr, 1 Zr, 1 large heart, 2 small hearts
¼ yd.	Light Print	background	3 A, 5 KK, 1 S, 1 Z, 2 Zr, 1 I, 1 B, 1 L, 1 M, 1 Wr
⅛ yd.	Med. Peach Solid	face, body, legs	1 T, 1 RR, 1 A, 1 GG, 1 B, 2 KK, 1 AAr
⅛ yd.	Light Peach Solid	arms	3 GGr, 2 KK
⅛ yd.*	Yellow/Gold Print	wing	1 wing
⅛ yd.*	Gold Print	hair	1 hair piece
⅛ yd.*	Gold Print	bow	1 bow
⅛ yd.	Red Print	hearts, arrow point	1 D, 1 large heart, 2 small hearts, 1 arrow point
½ yd.	Light Solid	lining	30" x 15"

*only a very small amount is needed: see pattern(s) for size

Also Needed: 12" of ½"-wide blue ribbon for bow tie, 2 ¾" pink buttons for hearts, 2 ¾" red buttons for hearts, 2 ¼" blue buttons for eyes, black embroidery floss for eyebrows, red embroidery floss for mouth and bow, gold embroidery floss for arrow, 30" x 15" batting

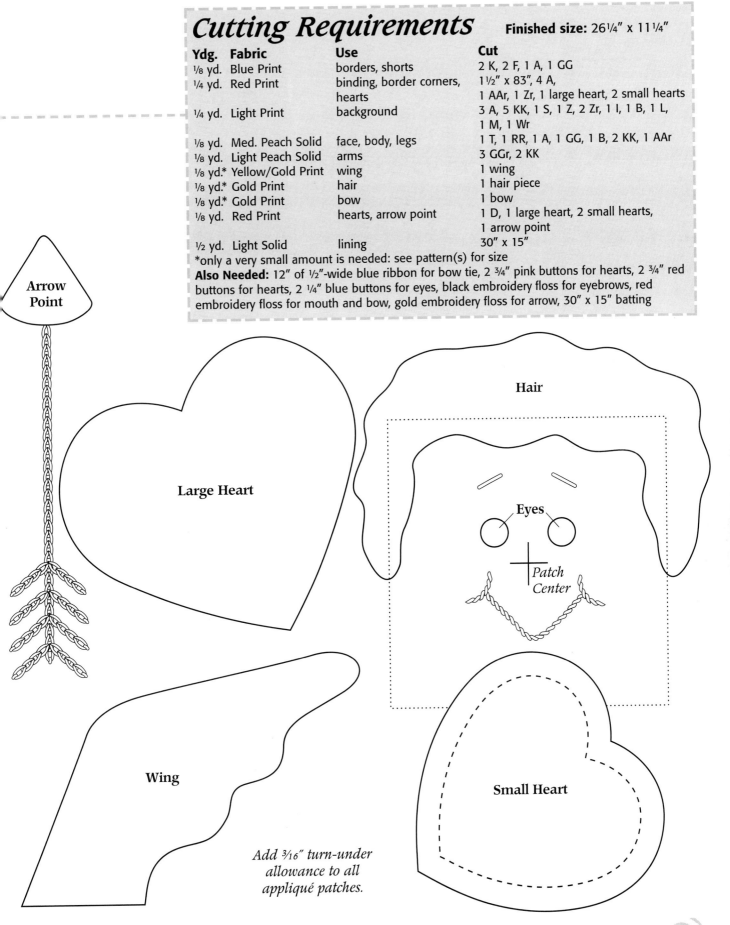

Arrow Point

Large Heart

Hair

Eyes

Patch Center

Wing

Small Heart

Add ³⁄₁₆" turn-under allowance to all appliqué patches.

Raggedy Ann & Andy

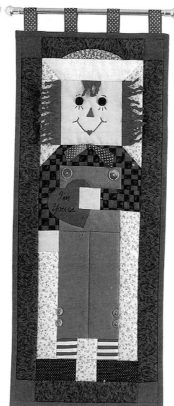

Color photos are on page 37.

Raggedy Ann

Raggedy Andy

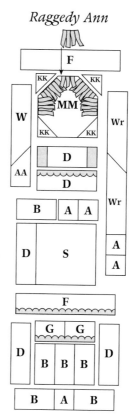

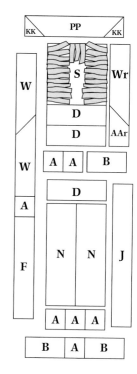

Piecing Diagrams

= 3-D piecing or appliqué

Who would ever guess that Raggedy Ann and Raggedy Andy are 50 years old? They look even cuter now than ever, especially with their button eyes and knotted hair. Make them for yourself, for a special young friend or for a Valentine's Day gift. They are the perfect way to say, "I Love You."

Assembly

1 Both: Lay out all patches as shown in the piecing diagrams.

2 Both: Use ½" x 5" strips for hair; these strips will be knotted and trimmed later as explained on page 12. Strips should overlap somewhat.

Ann: Sew background KK patches to two lower edges of MM (face) patch. Place six hair strips face down along each remaining long edge of face as shown below, positioning edges of strips at beginning and end of seam line.

Add remaining background KK patches and press seam allowances toward the face. Place five strips face down along each side of face.

Place three strips right side up (for bangs) at top of face plus four strips right side down. Baste strips.

Andy: Place 12 strips face down along each side of S (face), positioning edges of strips at beginning and end of seam. Place three strips

10

Cutting Requirements: Raggedy Ann

Finished size: 11¼" x 26¼"

Ydg.	Fabric	Use	Cut
⅛ yd.	Blue Print	borders	2 K, 2 F
¼ yd.	Red Print	binding, border corners, hair, heart	1½" x 83", 4 A, 29 strips ½" x 5", 1 heart
⅛ yd.	Light Yellow Print	background	1 F, 1 W, 1 Wr, 4 KK, 2 D, 1 B, 1 A
¼ yd.	Light Pink Solid	face, hands	1 MM, 2 A
⅛ yd.*	Red Solid	nose	1 nose
⅛ yd.	Med. Blue Print	dress	2 D, 1 A, 1 F
⅛ yd.	Light Blue Print	sleeves	1 AA, 1 B, 1 Wr
¼ yd.	White Print	apron, pantaloons	3 A, 1 D, 1 S, 2 G
⅛ yd.*	Red/White Stripe	stockings	2 B
⅛ yd.*	Black Print	shoes	2 B
½ yd.	Light Solid	lining	15" x 30"

*only a very small amount is needed: see pattern(s) for size

Also Needed: 2 ⅝" black buttons for eyes, ⅝ yd. of ¼"-wide white lace, black embroidery floss for eyes and heart, red embroidery floss for mouth, 15" x 30" batting

Cutting Requirements: Raggedy Andy

Finished size: 11¼" x 26¼"

Ydg.	Fabric	Use	Cut
⅛ yd.	Blue Print	borders	2 K, 2 F
¼ yd.	Red Print	binding, border corners, hair, heart	1½" x 83", 4 A, 27 strips ½" x 5", 1 heart
⅛ yd.	Light Yellow Print	background	2 KK, 1 W, 1 Wr, 1 F, 1 J, 2 A
¼ yd.	Light Pink Solid	face, hands	1 S, 2 A
⅛ yd.*	Light Blue Print	top of hat	1 top of hat
⅛ yd.	White Print	hat	1 PP
⅛ yd.*	Red Solid	nose	1 nose
⅛ yd.	Red/Blue Check	shirt	1 W, 1 D, 1 AAr, 1 B
⅛ yd.	Blue Solid	overalls	2 D, 1 A, 2 N
⅛ yd.*	Red/White Stripe	socks	2 A
⅛ yd.*	Black Print	shoes	2 B
½ yd.	Light Solid	lining	15" x 30"

*only a very small amount is needed: see pattern(s) for size

Also Needed: 2 ⅝" black buttons for eyes, 2 ¾" gold buttons for overalls, 4 ½" gold buttons for legs, 9" of 1"-wide blue ribbon for tie, black embroidery floss for eyes and heart, red embroidery floss for mouth, 15" x 30" batting

---

right side up (for bangs) at top of face. Baste strips.

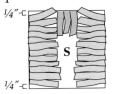

3 Ann: To make her apron straps, fold two white print A patches in half with wrong sides together. Baste to a medium blue print D patch, matching raw edges.

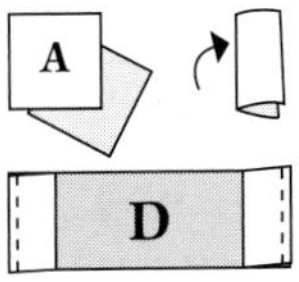

4 Ann: As shown in the piecing diagram, add lace to patches so it will be caught in the seams.

Both: Join lettered patches as shown in the piecing diagrams. Wherever possible, press seam allowances toward Ann or Andy. When piecing the hand, press all seam allowances (except the ones with the sleeve) toward the hand. For the hand/sleeve seam, press allowances toward the sleeve.

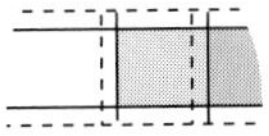

5 Both: Using two ply of black floss,

embroider lines around eyes and the lettering on the heart in outline stitch or backstitch. Using three ply of red floss, embroider mouth lines in chain stitch and embroider the heart in satin stitch.

6 Both: Appliqué the nose. Baste the heart

in place, partially covering the hand. Appliqué the heart except where it overlaps the hand.

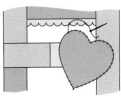

Before finishing appliquéing the heart,

work on the wrong side to open the seams around three sides of the hand.

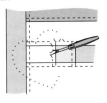

Pull the hand patch through to lie on top of

the heart; baste the hand in place. Appliqué the hand over the heart. Trim away the heart where it lies underneath the hand so it won't show through.

7 Andy: Appliqué light blue print top of hat to one blue print F border as shown here.

Both: Referring to the

general instructions, add border strips and corner squares. Press seam allowances toward the borders.

8 Both: Referring to the general instructions, assemble lining, batting and quilt top. Quilt in-the-ditch as shown in the quilting diagrams. Bind quilts.

9 Both: Sew on black buttons for eyes. **Andy:** Sew on gold buttons for overalls and legs.

10 Both: Referring to the information

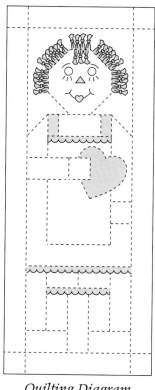

Quilting Diagram

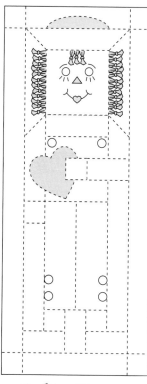

Quilting Diagram

below, tie knots in hair and trim the ends.

11 Andy: Tie ribbon with overhand

knot and tack to quilt at neck. We used ribbon tabs for Raggedy Ann and Raggedy Andy; see page 77 for information.

Raggedy Hair Styling

Once Raggedy Ann and Andy have their hair sewn in place, you will notice that they really need a cut and "perm." Don't worry! Our little friends will look great in no time at all.

Please wait until after the quilting and binding are finished before styling Ann and Andy's hair. The strips will be a little raveled, but that is part of their raggedy look.

The reason why we called for strips 5" long

is that this generous length will make it much easier to tie each strip in a knot. The knot to use is called an overhand knot, and it is made like this.

Tie each strip with an overhand knot. Pull knots tightly so they won't come undone. For bangs, knots can be

about ¾" from the seam; for other strips, knots can be about 1¼" from the seam. After tying all strips, trim each one about ⅜" from the knot.

¾"	⅜"

Bangs

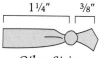

1¼"	⅜"

Other Strips

Since hair spray does not work very well for fabric hair, Raggedy Ann will need a little help to keep her hair out of her eyes. Using a single strand of red thread and working from the back of the quilt, take one tiny hand-sewn stitch to tack a strand of hair to the quilt. You can either tack every strand of hair or you can sew just the 16 at the top of her head. If Raggedy Andy's hair droops, of course you can tack his as well.

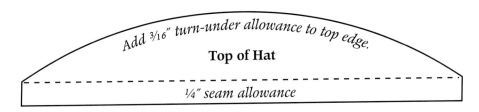

Add 3/16" turn-under allowance to top edge.

Top of Hat

¼" seam allowance

Eye   Nose   Eye

Patch Center

Ann's Face

Trace this heart/mouth for Ann and Andy.

Eye   Nose   Eye

Patch Center

Andy's Face

Ann's Heart

Add 3/16" turn-under allowance to all appliqué patches.

Be Mine

Andy's Heart

I'm Yours

Irish Jig

Catch him if you can! Our mischievous leprechaun is dancing a jig and leading the way to a pot o' gold. Many people claim to be Irish around St. Patrick's Day, and a little bit o' blarney is to be expected. But those who have a genuine claim to Irish heritage might want to adopt this fellow as a happy year-'round friend.

Assembly

1 Lay out all patches as shown in the piecing diagram.

2 Join lettered patches as shown in the piecing diagram. (Find directions for sewing set-in patches on page 30.) Wherever possible, press seam allowances toward the leprechaun.

3 Appliqué eyebrows and cheeks. Appliqué large gold buckle patches on hat and small gold

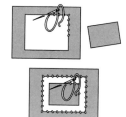

buckle patches on shoes. Appliqué black buckle center patches over gold buckles.

Appliqué shamrock stem, opening seams as necessary to tuck in the ends. Close seams with a few hand stitches.

4 Using three ply of red floss, embroider mouth in outline stitch.

5 Referring to the general instructions, add border strips and corner squares. Press seam allowances toward borders.

6 Appliqué black ribbon pipe stem and gold print pipe bowl. The pipe bowl will overlap the border and the pipe stem.

7 Referring to the general instructions, assemble lining, batting and quilt top. Quilt in-the-ditch as shown in the quilting diagram. Bind the quilt. Add tabs or sleeve if desired; see page 77 for information.

8 Add ½" button eyes and sew ⅞" buttons in place on shirt.

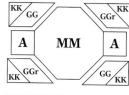

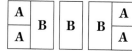

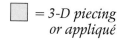

Piecing Diagram

[ ] = 3-D piecing or appliqué

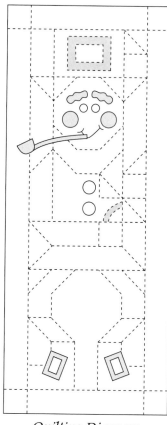

Quilting Diagram

Cutting Requirements

Finished size: 11¼" x 26¼"

Ydg.	Fabric	Use	Cut
⅛ yd.	Blue Print	borders	2 K, 2 F
¼ yd.	Light Green Print	binding, border corners	1½" x 83", 4 A
¼ yd.	Light Gold Print	background	2 B, 10 KK, 1 SS, 3 A, 1 MM
¼ yd.	Tan Solid	face, hands	1 MM, 1 KK, 1 A
⅛ yd.	Rust Print	hair, eyebrows, beard	4 KK, 1 eyebrow & 1 reversed, 1 FF
⅛ yd.	Black Solid	hat, boots, buckle centers	1 M, 2 KK, 2 A, 2 B, 1 large hat buckle center, 2 small shoe buckle centers
⅛ yd.*	Peach Solid	cheeks	2 cheeks
⅛ yd.	Med. Green Print	sleeves	1 A, 1 JJr, 2 Z
⅛ yd.	Med. Green Print	shirt	3 KK, 1 T, 1 A, 1 PP
⅛ yd.	Dark Green Print	shamrock, pants	3 A, 2 KK, 1 stem, 1 GG, 1 GGr
⅛ yd.*	Green/Gold Stripe	leggings	1 GG, 1 GGr
⅛ yd.	Gold Print	pipe, buckles	1 pipe bowl, 1 large hat buckle, 2 small shoe buckles
½ yd.	Light Solid	lining	15" x 30"

*only a very small amount is needed: see pattern(s) for size

Also Needed: 4" of ¼"-wide black ribbon for pipe stem, 2 ½" black buttons for eyes, 2 ⅞" gold buttons for shirt, red embroidery floss for mouth, 15" x 30" batting

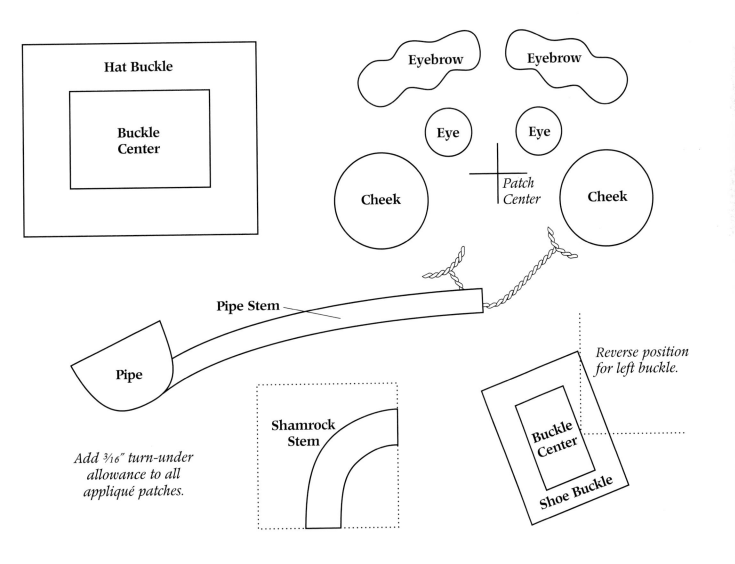

Hat Buckle

Buckle Center

Eyebrow

Eyebrow

Eye

Eye

Patch Center

Cheek

Cheek

Pipe Stem

Pipe

Reverse position for left buckle.

Shamrock Stem

Buckle Center

Shoe Buckle

Add ³⁄₁₆" turn-under allowance to all appliqué patches.

Easter Bunny

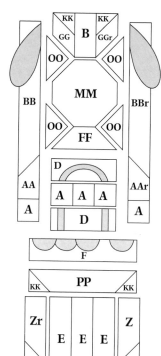

Color photo is on page 38.

This dapper fellow is more complex than some of the quilts in this book, but isn't he worth it? If you want some extra help, find information about 3-D piecing in the Special Techniques (pages 4 and 5). Information and stitch diagrams for embroidery are on pages 75 and 76.

Assembly

1 Lay out all patches as shown in the piecing diagram.

2 To make ears, sew an ear and ear reversed (right sides together) around curved edge, stopping at circle. Clip to dot as shown below. Turn right side out and press flat. Repeat for other ear. Baste ears to BB and BBr patches as shown in the piecing diagram, allowing ¼" at top for border seam.

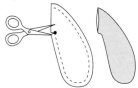

To make eggs, sew two egg patches (right sides together) around curved edge. Turn right side out and press flat. Repeat for other eggs. Baste eggs to F patch as shown in the diagram below, leaving a ½" space where the handle will go and allowing ¼" at ends of F for seams.

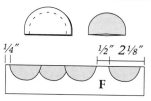

3 Read directions for set-in patches on page 30. Join lettered patches as shown in the piecing diagram. Wherever possible, press seam allowances toward the Easter bunny or basket.

4 Appliqué eyes, nose, bow lining, bow patch and bow patch reversed, bow knot, pink solid flower, chicks and chicks' beaks. Appliqué basket handle patches, opening seams as necessary to tuck in ends. Close seams.

Piecing Diagram

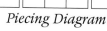 = 3-D piecing or appliqué

5 To make 3-D flower, sew flower and flower reversed (with right sides together) around edge. Clip indentations. Carefully cut a small slit in one layer only. Turn flower right side out through slit. Press flat. Tack flower to basket. Appliqué both flower centers, sewing through all layers.

6 Referring to the general instructions, add border strips and corner squares. Press seam allowances toward the borders.

7 Use three ply floss for all embroidery. Using black floss, embroider whiskers in outline stitch and make chicks' eyes with three french knots. With pink floss, embroider mouth in chain stitch. Using orange floss, embroider one chick's legs in chain stitch.

8 Referring to the general instructions, assemble lining, batting and quilt top. Quilt in-the-ditch as shown in the quilting diagram. Bind the quilt. Add tabs or sleeve if desired; see page 77 for information.

9 Add buttons for eyes.

Cutting Requirements

Finished size: 11¼" x 26¼"

Ydg.	Fabric	Use	Cut
⅛ yd.	Multi Print	borders	2 K, 2 F
¼ yd.	Pink/White Plaid	binding, border corners, bow	1½" x 83", 4 A, 1 bow patch & 1 reversed
⅛ yd.	Light Pink Print	background	1 BB, 1 BBr, 4 KK, 1 B, 4 OO, 2 A, 1 Z, 1 Zr, 1 E
¼ yd.	Med. Purple Print	bunny's body	1 GG, 1 GGr, 1 MM, 1 FF, 2 D, 2 AA, 2 AAr, 1 A, 2 E
⅛ yd.	Light Purple Print	bunny's ears and hands	2 ear patches & 2 reversed, 2 A
⅛ yd.*	Light Pink Print	bunny's eyes	2 eyes
⅛ yd.	Dark Pink Solid	bow lining and knot, nose, flower	1 bow lining & 1 reversed, 1 knot, 1 nose, 1 flower
⅛ yd.	Yellow/Gold Print	basket	1 handle top, 2 handle sides, 1 F, 1 PP
⅛ yd.*	Pink Print	flower	1 flower & 1 reversed
⅛ yd.*	Lime Green Print	egg, flower center	2 egg patches, 1 flower center
⅛ yd.*	Med. Blue Print	egg	2 egg patches
⅛ yd.*	Orange Print	egg	2 egg patches
⅛ yd.*	Purple Print	egg	2 egg patches
⅛ yd.*	Orange Print	flower center	1 flower center
⅛ yd.*	Yellow Check	chicks	1 chick & 1 reversed
⅛ yd.*	Orange Print	chicks' beaks	2 chick beaks
½ yd.	Light Solid	lining	15" x 30"

*only a very small amount is needed: see pattern(s) for size

Also Needed: 2 ⅜" blue buttons for eyes, black embroidery floss for bunny's whiskers and chicks' eyes, pink embroidery floss for bunny's mouth, orange embroidery floss for chick's legs, 15" x 30" batting

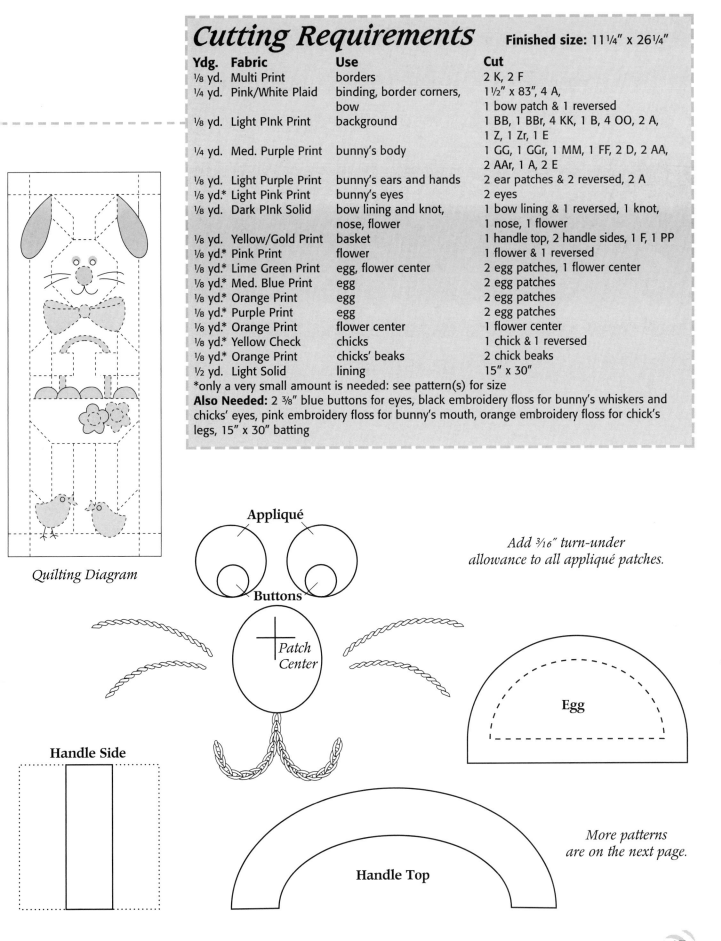

Quilting Diagram

Appliqué

Buttons

Patch Center

Add 3/16" turn-under allowance to all appliqué patches.

Egg

Handle Side

Handle Top

More patterns are on the next page.

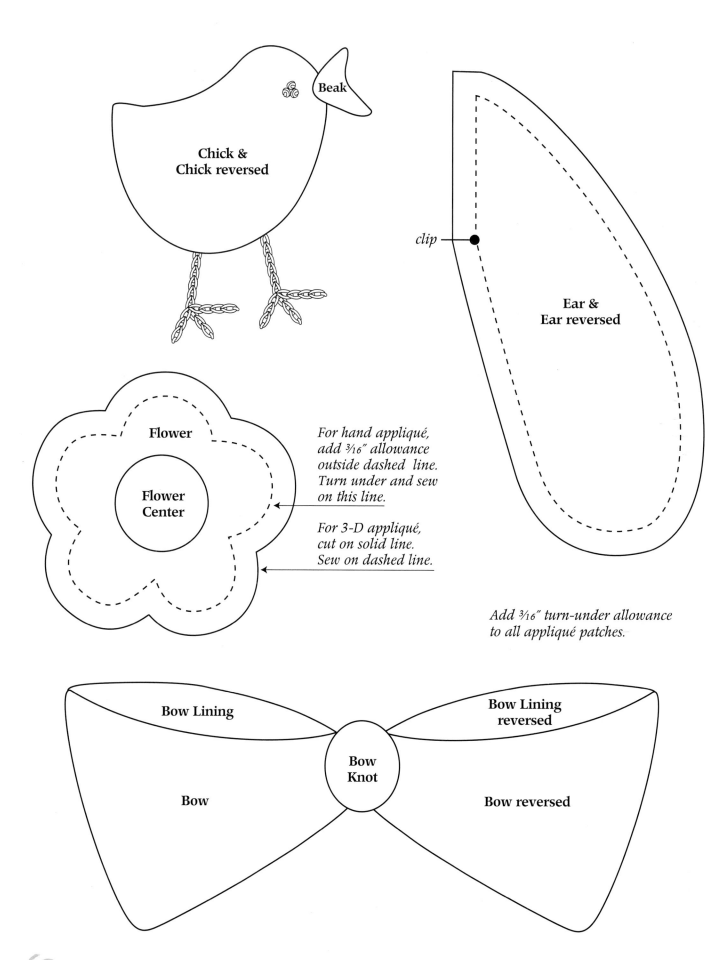

Chick &
Chick reversed

Beak

Ear &
Ear reversed

clip

Flower

Flower
Center

For hand appliqué, add ³⁄₁₆" allowance outside dashed line. Turn under and sew on this line.

For 3-D appliqué, cut on solid line. Sew on dashed line.

Add ³⁄₁₆" turn-under allowance to all appliqué patches.

Bow Lining

Bow Lining
reversed

Bow
Knot

Bow

Bow reversed

May Basket

Color photo is on page 38.

Assembly

1 Lay out all patches as shown in the piecing diagram on the next page.

2 The upright parts of the basket handle are made with folded patches that are sewn over background patches. Fold the tan check C and E patches in half lengthwise with wrong sides together. Referring to diagrams at right, position a folded C on a pastel FF, a folded C on a pastel AA, a folded E on a pastel Wr, and a folded E on a pastel PP, matching raw edges. Pin or baste. Trim ends of Cs and Es to match the shapes of the pastel patches.

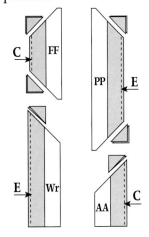

3 Join lettered patches as shown in the piecing diagram. Wherever possible, press seam allowances toward the basket or bow.

4 To make stems, fold bias strips in half lengthwise with wrong sides together; sew ⅛" from raw edge.

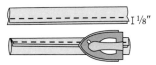

Bias strips

Turn under raw edge ¼" and press. Trim seam allowances just outside

The tradition of delivering May Baskets early in the morning on May Day is a delightful ritual of spring. Lilacs, tulips, spirea and other flowers and greens are tucked into paper baskets (often with the stems wrapped in a wad of aluminum foil). The best part is ringing the doorbell and hiding in the bushes (without giggling!) while the recipient opens the door to find the surprise gift. If this tradition has faded in your part of the country, revive it with this quilt–even if it causes you to giggle.

Cutting Requirements

Finished size: 11¼" x 26¼"

Ydg.	Fabric	Use	Cut
⅛ yd.	Teal Print	borders, stems, leaf	2 K, 2 F, bias strip 1½" x 4" for stem, 1 leaf
¼ yd.	Dark Pink Print	binding, border corners, bow	1½" x 83", 5 A, 2 FF, 1 each bow tail
⅛ yd.	Light Yellow Print	background around basket	1 Z, 1 Zr, 1 FF, 1 DD, 1 DDr, 2 A
⅛ yd.	Pastel Floral Print	background inside basket	1 FF, 1 JJr, 1 H, 1 II, 1 PP, 1 W, 1 Wr, 1 AA, 1 AAr
¼ yd.	Tan Check	basket	1 GG, 1 GGr, 2 C, 2 E, 1 TT, 1 D
⅛ yd.	Yellow Print	flower, flower centers	1 Q, 1 Qr, 1 large flower center, 2 small flower centers
⅛ yd.	Gold Print	flower centers	2 small flower centers
⅛ yd.	Pink Print	flower	1 Q, 1 Qr
⅛ yd.	White Print	flowers	4 small flowers
⅛ yd.	Purple Print	flower	1 large flower
⅛ yd.*	Med. Peach Print	flower	2 small flowers
⅛ yd.*	Light Peach Print	flower	2 small flowers
⅛ yd.	Med. Green Print	stems, leaves	bias strip 1½" x 9" for stems, 3 leaves
½ yd.	Light Solid	lining	15" x 30"

*only a very small amount is needed: see pattern(s) for size
Also Needed: 6 ⅜" red buttons, 15" x 30" batting

19

the sewn line. Cut off stem pieces as needed.

5 Appliqué stems as shown in diagram below. Appliqué leaves and large flower.

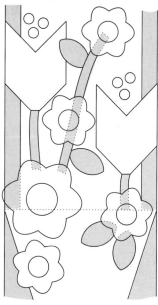

6 Appliqué bow tails, opening seam at the bottom of the dark pink A patch and tucking in the ends. Close the seam with hand sewing.

7 Referring to the general instructions, add

border strips and corner squares. Press seam allowances toward the borders.

8 Make 3-D flowers by placing two small flower patches right sides together; sew around edge. (See page 21 for some tips on using Con-Tact® paper to help make 3-D flowers.) Clip seam allowances at indentations. Carefully cut a small slit in one layer of the flower, and turn the flower through the slit. Press flat. Repeat to make a total of four 3-D flowers. Tack flowers to quilt. Appliqué flower centers over large and small flowers.

9 Referring to the general instructions, assemble lining, batting and quilt top. Quilt in-the-ditch as shown in the quilting diagram. Bind the quilt. Add tabs or sleeve if desired; see page 77 for information. Sew red buttons to quilt.

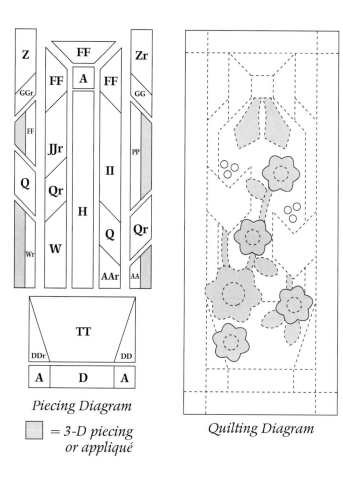

Piecing Diagram

☐ = *3-D piecing or appliqué*

Quilting Diagram

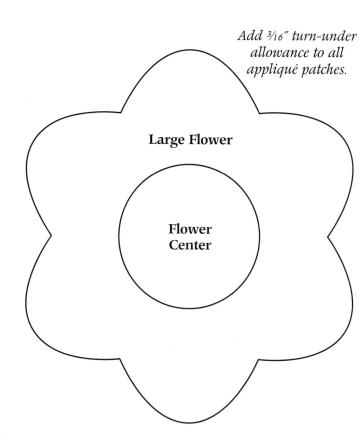

Add ³⁄₁₆″ turn-under allowance to all appliqué patches.

Large Flower

Flower Center

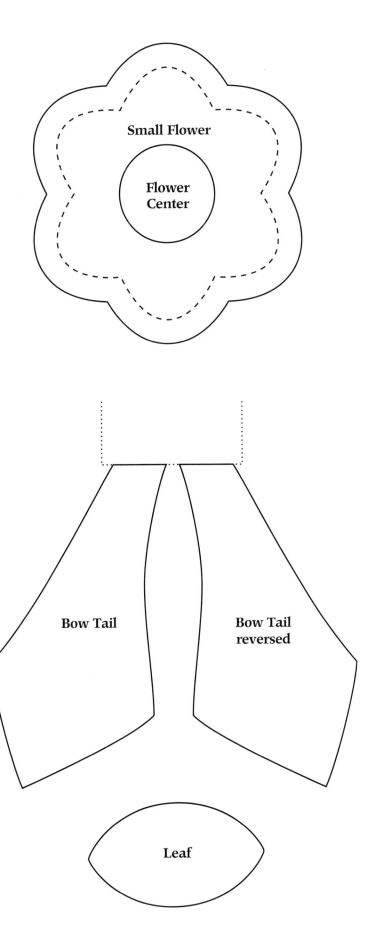

Making 3-D Appliqués

There is an easy way to have an accurate seam line without marking patches. The secret is Con-Tact® paper, which is available at discount and hardware stores.

1 Select clear or solid white Con-Tact paper so you will be able to see through it to trace the pattern. You won't need very much.

2 Trace and cut out the shape to be sewn, but do not include seam allowances. Peel off the backing.

3 Cut 2 pieces of fabric a little larger than the appliqué. Put them right sides together. Pin them if they are larger than a few inches.

4 Adhere Con-Tact paper shape to fabric. Sew around the edge of the Con-Tact paper. A short stitch length will help you make smooth curves and a sturdy seam.

5 Remove Con-Tact paper and save it to use again if needed. One piece will make all four 3-D flowers for May Basket.

6 Trim one seam allowance to ⅛″, and trim the other a little wider or narrower.

7 Clip each indentation or inside (concave) curve. Cut a small slit for turning on the back side.

8 Turn right side out. Hemostats or tweezers are great for this. Use a pin or needle and your fingers to gently pull the appliqué into the correct shape with smooth curves. Press flat.

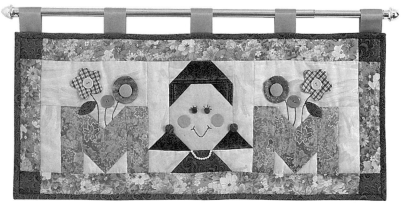

Color photo is on page 39.

I ♥ Mom

Show Mom how much you love her with this quilt. The best part is that you can select fabrics to match her hair, skin and favorite outfit. You could even give her embroidered glasses. Then add button-and-bead "jewelry" to match her personal style.

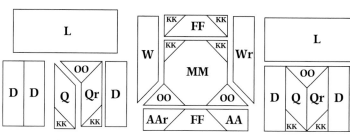

Piecing Diagram

Assembly

1 Lay out all patches as shown in the piecing diagram.

2 Join lettered patches as shown in the piecing diagram. Wherever possible, press seam allowances toward the M letters or toward Mom. If necessary, trim dark seam allowances to prevent them from showing through lighter fabric.

3 Appliqué leaves and cheeks.

4 Use three ply floss for all embroidery. Use green floss and outline stitch to embroider stems. With red floss and outline stitch, embroider mouth. Use blue floss and single straight stitches to embroider eyelashes.

5 Referring to the general instructions, add border strips and corner squares. Press seam allowances toward the borders.

6 Referring to the general instructions, assemble lining, batting and quilt top. Quilt in-the-ditch as shown in the quilting diagram. Bind the quilt. Add fabric tabs or sleeve if desired; see page 77 for information. Our quilt uses ribbon tabs; see the tip on the next page.

7 Make 3-D flowers as follows. Place petal flower and reversed petal flower right sides together. Sew around edge. Carefully cut a small slit in one layer, and turn the flower through the slit. Press flat. Repeat for other petal flower and two round flowers.

Sew flowers to quilt (with slit sides touching quilt), stitching through buttons and all layers.

Sew 1″ light orange buttons to tops of short stems. To make earrings, follow directions that come with covered buttons to cover two buttons with purple print. Sew earrings in place. For pearl necklace, use strong thread and tie a knot in one end. Stitch through the quilt from the back and string about 2¼″ of pearls on thread. Secure end of necklace with a couple of backstitches. Take a couple of stitches through the quilt to hold the necklace in place. We wouldn't want Mom to lose her pearls!

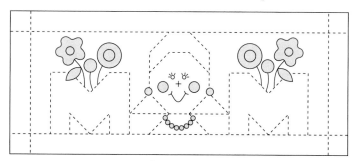

Quilting Diagram

Cutting Requirements

Finished size: 26¼" x 11¼"

Ydg.	Fabric	Use	Cut
⅛ yd.	Pink/Multi Print	borders	2 K, 2 F
¼ yd.	Purple Print	binding, border corners, earrings, blouse	1½" x 83", 4 A, 2 circles to cover buttons for earrings, 1 FF
⅛ yd.	Pastel Print	background	2 L, 2 D, 2 OO, 6 KK, 1 W, 1 Wr, 1 AA, 1 AAr
⅛ yd.	Pink Print	M letters	4 D, 2 Q, 2 Qr
¼ yd.	Light Pink Solid	face	1 MM
⅛ yd.*	Med. Pink Solid	cheeks	2 cheeks
⅛ yd.	Brown Print	hair	1 FF, 2 KK, 2 OO
⅛ yd.*	Pink Plaid	flowers	2 petal flowers & 2 reversed
⅛ yd.*	Blue Print	flowers	4 round flowers
⅛ yd.*	Green Print	leaves	2 leaves
½ yd.	Light Solid	lining	30" x 15"

*only a very small amount is needed: see pattern(s) for size

Also Needed: 2 ⅝" yellow buttons, 2 1" light orange buttons, 2 ⅞" pink buttons, 2 ½" covered buttons for earrings, 2 ⅜" blue buttons for eyes, green embroidery floss for stems, blue embroidery floss for eyes, red embroidery floss for mouth, 4mm pearls, 30" x 15" batting

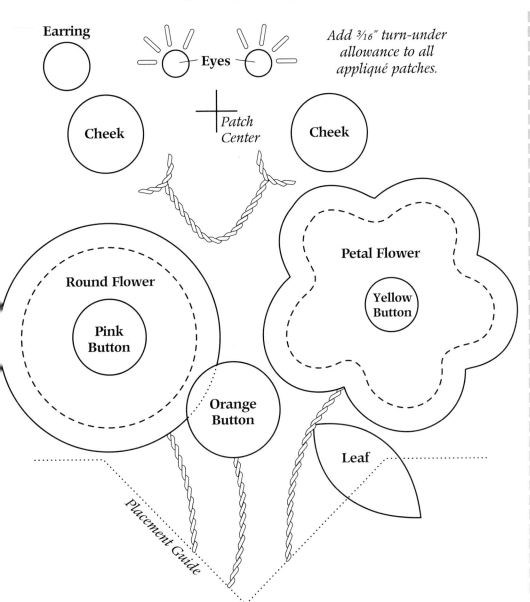

Earring

Eyes

Add ³⁄₁₆" turn-under allowance to all appliqué patches.

Cheek   + *Patch Center*   Cheek

Petal Flower

Round Flower   Yellow Button

Pink Button   Orange Button   Leaf

Placement Guide

Making Ribbon Tabs

Fabric tabs are easy to make (and instructions can be found on page 77), but ribbon tabs are even easier.

1 We used pink satin ribbon that is 1½" wide, and we made 5 tabs. Each one takes 5" of ribbon, so we used a little under ¾ yard.

2 To make the tabs, cut the ends of ribbon with pinking shears, fold each one in half and pin them to the back of the quilt. Our tabs extend above the quilt by 1¾". Pin all tabs in place.

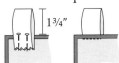

1¾"

3 Sew tabs to the quilt with hand sewing or use invisible thread and machine stitch in-the-ditch in the binding seam through all layers.

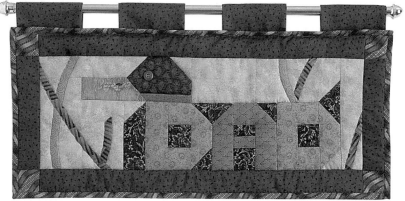

Color photo on page 39.

Dear Old Dad

> There is no role in a man's life that is more important than being a good father. Show Dad how well he does by making a special quilt for his office or study. There is just one thing missing from our quilt: the signature of a loving child.

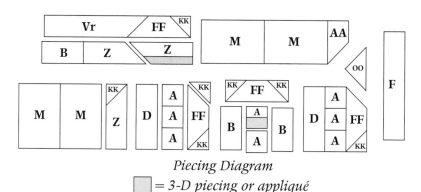

Piecing Diagram

 = 3-D piecing or appliqué

Assembly

1 Lay out all patches as shown in the piecing diagram.

2 For the duck's neck, first trim away ½" from one long edge of orange print C patch. Fold patch in half lengthwise (wrong sides together) and press. As shown below, position folded strip along edge of green print Z, matching raw edges. Baste C patch in place, sewing ⅛" from edge. Trim the end of the orange patch to match Z.

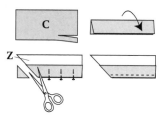

3 For the cross piece in the letter A, fold the medium brown print A patch in half and baste it to a dark brown print A patch as shown below. Appliqué folded edge of medium brown patch.

4 Join the lettered patches as shown in the piecing diagram. Wherever possible, press seam allowances toward the duck. If necessary, trim dark seam allowances to prevent them from showing through lighter fabric.

5 Appliqué reeds, working in numerical order and opening seams as necessary to tuck in ends. (Most of the ends will be caught in the border seams.)

6 Referring to the general instructions, add border strips and corner squares. Press seam allowances toward the borders.

7 Using three ply of dark brown floss, embroider nostril with a single lazy daisy stitch.

8 Referring to the general instructions, assemble lining, batting and quilt top. Quilt in-the-ditch as shown below. Bind the quilt. Add tabs or sleeve if desired; see page 77. Add button for eye.

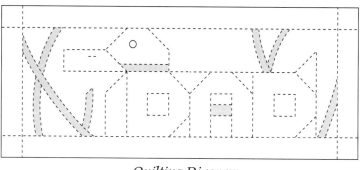

Quilting Diagram

Cutting Requirements

Finished size: 26¼" x 11¼"

Ydg.	Fabric	Use	Cut
⅛ yd.	Blue Print	borders	2 K, 2 F
¼ yd.	Teal/Blue Print	binding, border corners	1½" x 83", 4 A
⅛ yd.	Light Blue Print	background	1 Vr, 1 B, 4 M, 1 AA, 1 F, 3 KK
⅛ yd.*	Gold Print	duck's bill	1 Z
⅛ yd.*	Green Print	duck's head	1 FF, 1 Z
⅛ yd.*	Orange Print	duck's neck	1 C
⅛ yd.	Dark Brown Print	duck's body	1 Z, 4 KK, 1 OO, 4 A
⅛ yd.	Light Brown Print	D letters	2 D, 4 A, 2 FF
⅛ yd.	Med. Brown Print	A letter	1 FF, 2 B, 1 A
⅛ yd.	Lime Green Print	reeds	1 each reed nos. 1 and 5
⅛ yd.	Med. Green Print	reeds	1 each reed nos. 2, 3, 4 and 6
½ yd.	Light Solid	lining	30" x 15"

*only a very small amount is needed: see pattern(s) for size

Also Needed: ⅝" brown button for duck's eye, dark brown embroidery floss for duck's nostril, 30" x 15" batting

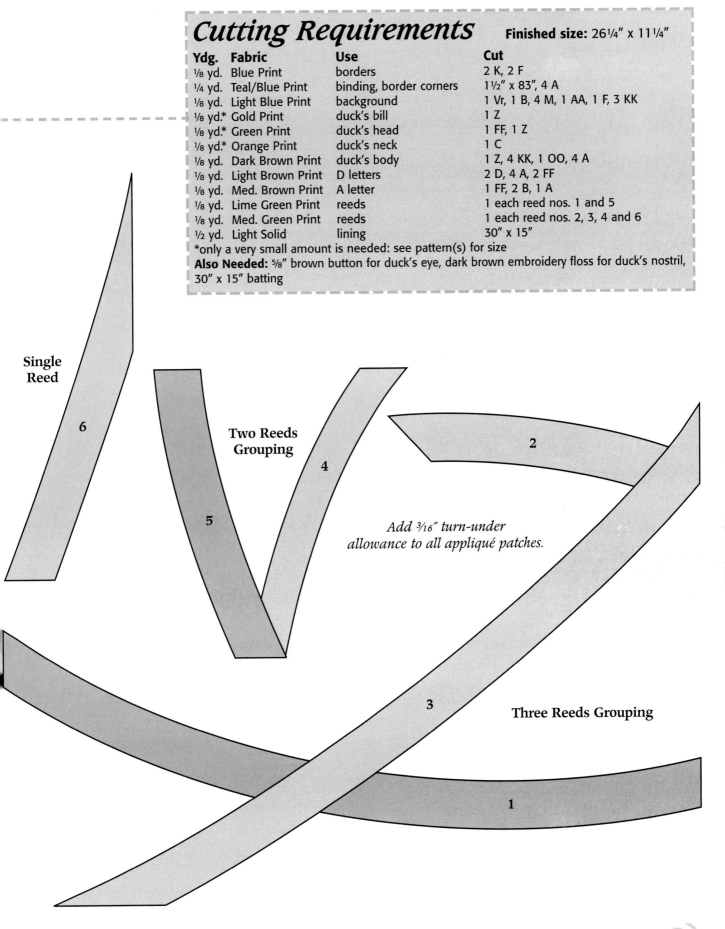

Single Reed

6

Two Reeds Grouping

4

2

5

Add ³⁄₁₆" turn-under allowance to all appliqué patches.

3

Three Reeds Grouping

1

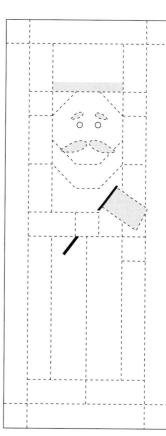

Color photo is on page 40.

Uncle Sam is proud to wave an American flag. We found fabric with many different sizes of flags printed on it and simply cut out the one we wanted (with turn-under allowances, of course). However, you can easily make a flag simply by following the directions on the next page.

Uncle Sam

Assembly

1 Lay out all patches as shown in the piecing diagram.

2 To make the hatband, fold blue print D patch in half lengthwise. As shown below, position folded strip along one edge of red/white stripe M, matching raw edges. Baste hatband in place, sewing 1/8" from edge of patch.

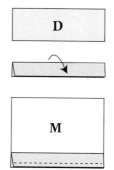

3 Join lettered patches as shown in the piecing diagram. Wherever possible, press seam allowances toward Uncle Sam. If necessary, trim dark seam allowances to prevent them from showing through lighter seam allowances.

4 Appliqué eyebrows and mustache. Appliqué ribbon flag handle, opening seams

as necessary to tuck in ends.

5 Referring to the general instructions, add border strips and corner squares. Press seam allowances toward the borders. Appliqué the flag, which will overlap the border.

6 Referring to the general instructions, assemble the lining, batting and quilt top. Quilt in-the-ditch as shown in the quilting diagram. Bind the quilt. Add tabs or sleeve if desired; see page 77 for information. Add buttons for Uncle Sam's eyes.

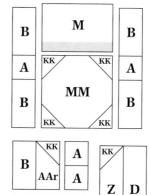

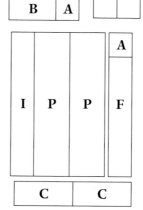

Piecing Diagram

☐ = 3-D piecing or appliqué

Quilting Diagram

Cutting Requirements

Finished size: 11¼" x 26¼"

Ydg.	Fabric	Use	Cut
⅛ yd.	Red Print	borders	2 K, 2 F
¼ yd.	Blue Print	binding, border corners, hatband	1½" x 83", 4 A, 1 D
⅛ yd.	Light Blue Print	background	4 B, 1 I, 1 F
¼ yd.	Flesh Solid	face, hands	1 MM, 2 A
⅛ yd.	White Print	hair, eyebrows, mustache, beard	6 KK, 1 eyebrow & 1 reversed, 1 each mustache patch, 1 A
⅜ yd.	Red/White Stripe	hat, pants	1 M, 2 P
⅛ yd.	Blue Print	hat, vest	3 A, 1 AAr, 1 Z
⅛ yd.	Blue/Gold Print	sleeves	2 B, 1 D
⅛ yd.	Black Solid	shoes	2 C
½ yd.	Light Solid	lining	15" x 30"

Also Needed: 2 ½" blue buttons for eyes, 3" of ¼"-wide black ribbon for flag, 2¾" x 1¾" flag or small flag cut from fabric (to appliqué) or see tip and pattern below, 15" x 30" batting

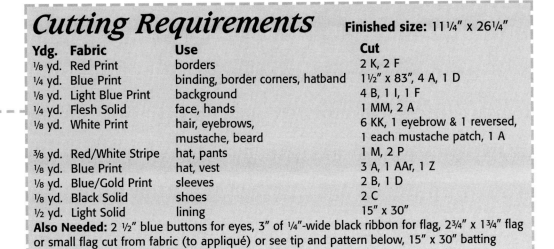

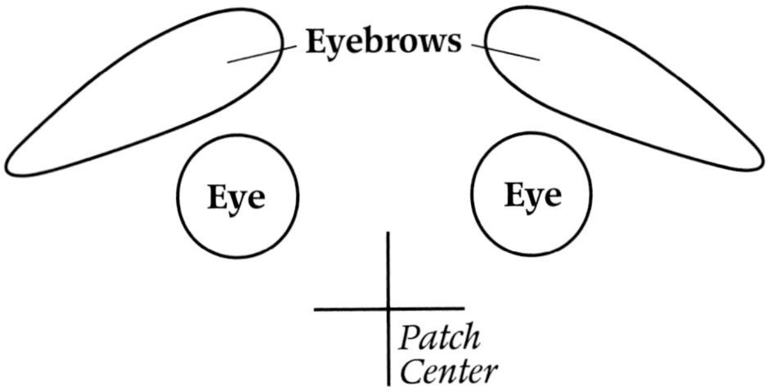

Eyebrows

Eye   **Eye**

Patch Center

Mustache

Add ³⁄₁₆" turn-under allowance to all appliqué patches.

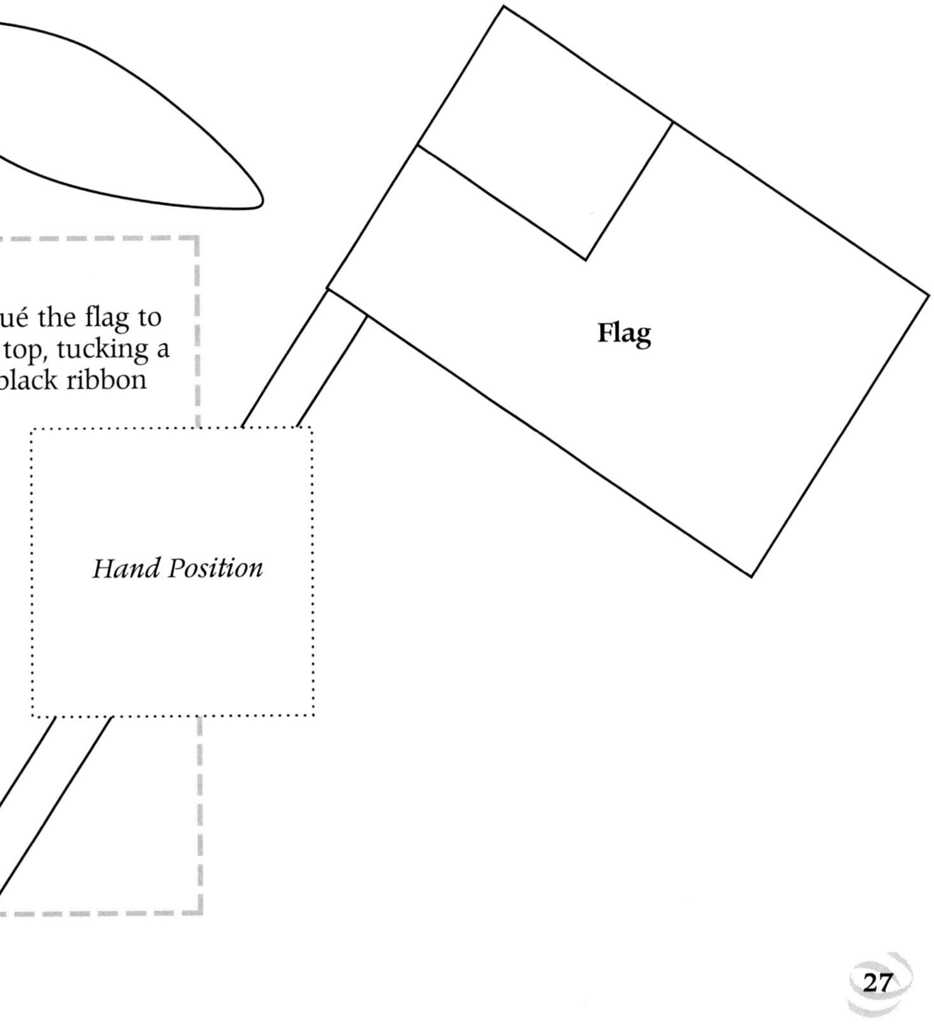

Flag

Hand Position

How To Make a Flag

Uncle Sam's flag can be any size you desire.

1 To make your own flag, simply use a small amount of red/white striped fabric. (The U.S. flag has a red stripe at the top and the bottom.) Cut a rectangle in the size you need, adding turn-under allowances.

2 Cut a small rectangle of blue fabric for the corner, again including turn-under allowances, and appliqué it to the striped fabric.

3 Appliqué the flag to the quilt top, tucking a piece of black ribbon underneath it for the flagpole.

4 Add white star-shaped beads or sequins.

Color photo is on page 39.

Old Glory

S	W	HH	V
	V	HH	W
	U	HH	Z

X	HH	AA
Y	HH	KK

Piecing Diagram

Assembly

1 Lay out all patches as shown in the piecing diagram.

2 Join lettered patches as shown in the piecing diagram. Press seam allowances to one side. If necessary, trim dark seam allowances to prevent them from showing through the light fabric.

3 Referring to the general instructions, add border strips and corner squares. Press seam allowances toward the borders.

4 Referring to the general instructions, assemble lining, batting and quilt top. Quilt in-the-ditch as shown in the quilting diagram. Bind the quilt. Add tabs

or sleeve if desired; see page 77 for information.

5 Make 3-D stars by placing two patches right sides together and sewing around edge. Carefully cut a small slit in one layer, and turn star right side out through the slit. Press flat. Repeat for other star. Sew each star to the quilt (with slit side touching quilt), stitching through a gold button and all layers.

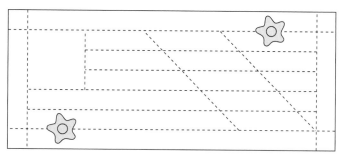

Quilting Diagram

A pattern for the 3-D Star is included with the Star-Spangled Cats on page 30.

Cutting Requirements
Finished size: 26¼" x 11¼"

Ydg.	Fabric	Use	Cut
⅛ yd.	Blue Print	borders	2 K, 2 F
¼ yd.	Red Print	binding, border corners	1½" x 83", 4 A
¼ yd.	Dark Blue Print	flag	1 S
⅛ yd.	Red/White Print	flag stripes	1 W, 1 V, 2 HH, 1 U, 1 Z, 1 Y, 1 KK
⅛ yd.	Off-White Print	flag stripes	3 HH, 1 V, 1 W, 1 X, 1 AA
⅛ yd.*	Blue/White Stripe	stars	2 stars and 2 reversed (see page 30)
½ yd.	Light Solid	lining	30" x 15"

*only a very small amount is needed: see pattern(s) for size
Also Needed: 2 ¾" gold buttons for stars, 30" x 15" batting

Star-Spangled Cats

Color photo is on page 40.

Cutting Requirements

Finished size: 11¼" x 26¼"

Ydg.	Fabric	Use	Cut
⅛ yd.	Blue/White Print	borders	2 K, 2 F
	(or ⅔ yd. if fabric has lengthwise design)		
¼ yd.	Red/White Stripe	binding, border corners	1½" x 83", 4 A
⅛ yd.	Yellow Print	background, two blocks	4 E, 2 FF, 4 KK, 2 AA, 2 AAr
⅛ yd.	Yellow/Gold Print	background, center block	2 E, 1 FF, 2 KK, 1 AA, 1 AAr
¼ yd.	Light Blue	cats' faces	3 MM
⅛ yd.	Dark Blue Print	cats' ears	6 OO
⅛ yd.	Red/White/Blue	cats' bodies	3 FF
⅛ yd.	Red/White Print	paws and tails	6 paws, 2 tails & 1 tail reversed
⅛ yd.*	Light Red Print	cats' noses	3 noses
⅛ yd.	Gold Print	stars	3 stars & 3 reversed
½ yd.	Light Solid	lining	15" x 30"

*only a very small amount is needed: see pattern(s) for size

Also Needed: 6 ½" blue buttons for cats' eyes, 3 ¾" star-shaped red buttons for stars, black embroidery floss for whiskers, red embroidery floss for mouths, 15" x 30" batting

These patriotic kitties look a little bit startled–maybe they just heard some firecrackers! The piecing goes super fast, and the appliqué and embroidery move right along. To see the nine-block version, turn the page.

Assembly

1 Lay out all patches as shown in the piecing diagram.

2 Join lettered patches as shown in the piecing diagram to make three blocks, but do not join the blocks yet. Wherever possible, press seam allowances toward the cats.

3 Appliqué paws and noses. The lower edges of paws need not be turned under because they will be caught in seams.

4 Using two ply of black floss, embroider whiskers in outline stitch or backstitch. With three ply of red floss, embroider mouths in chain stitch.

5 Join blocks. Referring to the general instructions, add border strips and corner squares. Press seam allowances toward the borders.

6 Appliqué tails, opening seams as necessary to tuck in ends of tails. Close seams.

7 Referring to the general instructions, assemble lining, batting and quilt top. Quilt in-the-ditch as shown in the quilting diagram on the next page. Bind the quilt. Add tabs or sleeve if desired; see page 77 for information.

8 To make the 3-D stars, sew a star patch and a star patch reversed with right sides together. Clip all inside curves. Carefully cut a small slit in one layer only. Turn star through slit. Press flat. Repeat to make two more stars like this. Tack the stars to the quilt with the slit sides touching quilt. Sew star-shaped buttons to the centers of stars, stitching through all the layers. Sew on buttons for the cats' eyes.

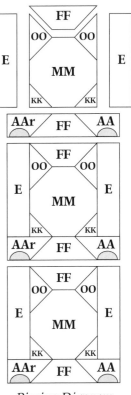

Piecing Diagram

▨ = 3-D piecing or appliqué

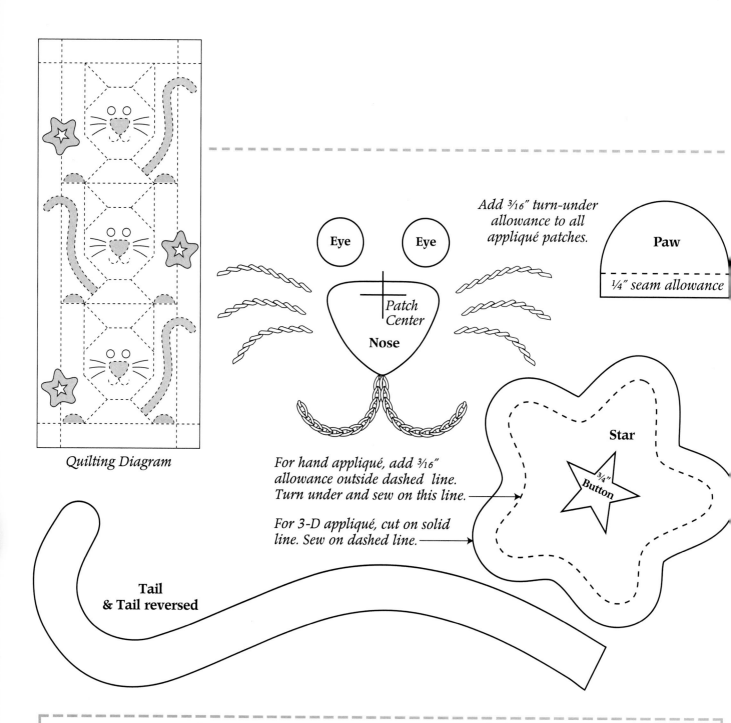

Quilting Diagram

Eye   Eye

Patch Center

Nose

Add ³⁄₁₆″ turn-under allowance to all appliqué patches.

Paw

¼″ seam allowance

For hand appliqué, add ³⁄₁₆″ allowance outside dashed line. Turn under and sew on this line. →

For 3-D appliqué, cut on solid line. Sew on dashed line. →

Star

³⁄₄″ Button

Tail & Tail reversed

Set-In Patches

Each cat block has one set-in patch (the FF above the head), and a few hints should make the sewing easy.

1 Sew the ears (OO patches) to the face (MM), but pay close attention to the best starting and stopping points for the seams. It is important to stop (or start) the line of sewing at the top of the face exactly at the end of the seam. It's a good idea to mark those spots on the wrong side of MM with a pencil.

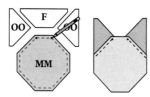

2 To stop on the mark, use the hand wheel to control the needle instead of using the foot pedal. Backstitch.

3 After sewing the ears, position the FF patch under the top of the head and sew between the dots.

4 Turn your work over and re-position FF to attach one ear, then the other.

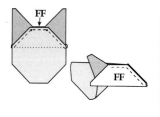

Cats' Meow

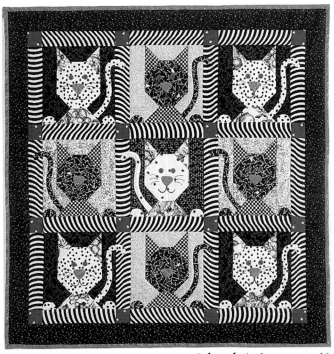

Color photo is on page 41.

Assembly

1 Lay out all patches as shown in the piecing diagram and the photo, noticing where various fabrics are placed.

2 Working one block at a time, join lettered patches as shown in the block-piecing diagram to make the nine blocks. Do not join blocks yet. Wherever possible, press seam allowances toward the cats.

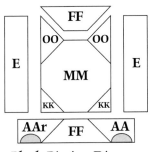

Block Piecing Diagram

☐ = 3-D piecing or appliqué

3 Appliqué paws and noses. The lower edges of paws need not be turned under because they will be caught in seams.

4 Using two ply of red floss or a single strand of pearl cotton, embroider whiskers in outline stitch or backstitch. With three ply of red floss or a single strand of pearl cotton, embroider mouths in chain stitch.

5 Lay out blocks as shown in the quilt piecing diagram on the next page. Working one row at a time, alternately join four black/white stripe sashes (F patches) and the blocks in the top row. Press the seam allowances toward the sashes. Repeat for middle and bottom rows. Appliqué tails, opening seams as necessary to tuck in ends. Close the seams.

6 Alternately join four red/white print setting squares (A patches)

Fabric Contrast

The fabrics we chose for our Cats' Meow quilt are all black and white (for blocks, sashes and borders) or red and white (for setting squares, cats' noses and binding). With a narrow color palette such as this one, high contrast is one of the keys to success. We selected fabric for backgrounds and faces/tails/paws that were either very light or very dark. Fabrics for ears and bodies and the striped sashes were about halfway between light and dark. A very dark border frames the quilt.

Cutting Requirements
Finished size: 33¼" x 33¼"

Ydg.	Fabric	Use	Cut
³⁄₈ yd.	Black/White Print	borders	2 borders 2½" x 35", 2 borders 2½" x 31"
½ yd.	Red/White Stripe	binding, noses	bias binding 1½" x 4⅛ yds., 9 noses
⅛ yd.	Red/White Print	setting squares	16 A
½ yd.	Black/White Stripe*	sashes	24 F
½ yd.	Black/White Darks*	cats and backgrounds	10 E, 5 FF, 10 KK, 5 AA, 5 AAr, 4 MM, 2 tails, 2 tails reversed, 8 paws
⅛ yd.	Black/White Meds.*	cats' ears, bodies	18 OO, 9 FF
½ yd.	Black/White Lights*	cats and backgrounds	8 E, 4 FF, 8 KK, 4 AA, 4 AAr, 5 MM, 4 tails, 1 tail reversed, 10 paws
1⅛ yds.	Light Solid	lining	37" x 37"

*see Fabric Notes in box above

Also Needed: 18 ½" red buttons for cats' eyes, red embroidery floss or no. 8 pearl cotton for mouths and whiskers, 37" x 37" batting

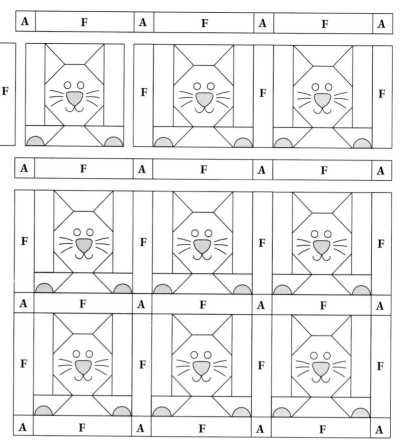

and three black/white stripe sashes (F patches). Press seam allowances toward the sashes. Repeat to make three more sash rows like this.

7 Alternately join cat-block rows and sash rows. Press the seam allowances toward the sashes. *Note:* Border dimensions include 2″ extra length for insurance. Pin borders to fit the quilt top and trim borders as necessary. Sew short border strips to sides of quilt top. Sew long borders to upper and lower edges of quilt top. Press seam allowances toward the borders.

8 Referring to the general instructions, assemble lining, batting and quilt top. Quilt in-the-ditch as shown in the quilting diagram. Bind the quilt. Add tabs or a sleeve if desired; see page 77 for information. Sew on button eyes.

Piecing Diagram

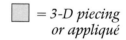 = *3-D piecing or appliqué*

Quilting Diagram

Summertime Picnic

Is your summertime livin' easy? Turn any day into a smiling summer holiday by making this quilt in either size. Hang one or both in your kitchen or breakfast nook. Or give a baby a happy start in life by making the nine-block version as a crib quilt.

Small Quilt Assembly

1 Lay out all patches as shown in the piecing diagram.

2 Join lettered patches as shown in the piecing diagram. Wherever possible, press seam allowances toward the sun, flowers, flowerpot or watermelon.

3 To make stems, fold green bias strip in half lengthwise with wrong sides together; sew 1/8" from raw edge. Turn under raw edge 1/4" and press. Trim seam allowance just outside sewn line. Cut off stem pieces as needed.

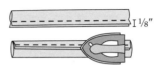

Bias strips

4 Appliqué stems, opening seams as necessary to tuck in ends. Close seams. Appliqué leaf, bee's wings, and bee's body.

5 See page 21 for a tip about making 3-D appliqués. To make 3-D flower, place flower patch and reversed flower patch right sides

Color photo is on page 40.

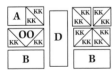
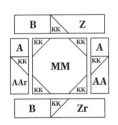
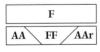
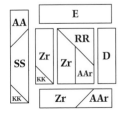

Piecing Diagram

Cutting Requirements: Small Quilt
Finished size: 11 1/4" x 26 1/4"

Ydg.	Fabric	Use	Cut
1/8 yd.	Multi Print	borders	2 K, 2 F
1/4 yd.	Green Print	binding, border corners, stems, leaf	1 1/2" x 83", 4 A, bias strip 1 1/4" x 6" for stems, 1 leaf
1/8 yd.	Lt. Yellow Print	background, sun block	2 B, 1 Z, 1 Zr, 2 A, 1 AA, 1 AAr
1/8 yd.	Lt. Blue Print	background, flowerpot	1 A, 6 KK, 1 D, 2 B, 1 AA, 1 AAr
1/8 yd.	Lt. Green Print	background, watermelon	1 AA, 1 AAr, 1 E, 1 RR, 1 D, 1 KK
1/4 yd.	Yellow Print	sun face, flower	1 MM, 1 flower & 1 reversed
1/8 yd.	Yellow Check	sun rays	8 KK
1/8 yd.*	Red Print	flower	1 KK
1/8 yd.*	Pink Print	flower	1 OO
1/8 yd.*	Blue Print	flower, bee's wings	2 KK, 2 bee's wings
1/8 yd.*	Purple Print	flower	3 KK
1/8 yd.*	Gold Print	flower center, bee's body	1 flower center, 1 bee's body
1/8 yd.	Rust Print no. 1	top of flowerpot	1 F
1/8 yd.*	Rust Print no. 2	bottom of flowerpot	1 FF
1/8 yd.	Green Print	watermelon	1 SS, 1 KK, 1 Zr
1/8 yd.*	Red Print	watermelon	1 Zr, 1 AAr
1/8 yd.*	Red Print	watermelon	1 Zr
1/2 yd.	Light Solid	lining	15" x 30"

*only a very small amount is needed: see pattern(s) for size

Also Needed: 2 1/4" black buttons for sun's eyes, red embroidery floss for sun's mouth, black embroidery floss for watermelon seeds and bee, 15" x 30" batting

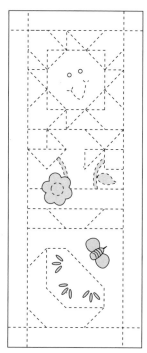

Quilting Diagram

together. Sew around edges. Clip all inside curves. Carefully cut a small slit in one layer of the flower, and turn the flower through the slit. Press flat. Tack flower to quilt. Appliqué flower center over flower.

6 Use three ply of floss for all embroidery. With red floss, embroider the sun's mouth in outline stitch or chain stitch. Using black floss,

embroider bee's body in outline stitch, and make the stinger with straight stitches. Add bee's eyes with black floss and french knots. For watermelon seeds, use black floss and lazy daisy stitches with smaller lazy daisy stitches inside, or use satin stitch.

7 Referring to the general instructions, add border strips and corner squares. Press seam

allowances toward the borders.

8 Referring to the general instructions, assemble lining, batting and quilt top. Quilt in-the-ditch as shown in the quilting diagram. Quilt the sun's rays in the background as shown. Bind the quilt. Add tabs or sleeve if desired; see page 77 for information. Add buttons for sun's eyes.

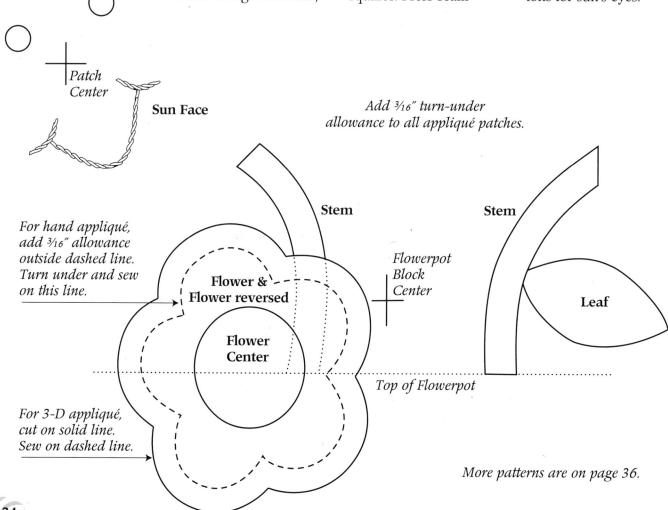

Patch Center

Sun Face

Add ³⁄₁₆″ turn-under allowance to all appliqué patches.

Stem

Stem

For hand appliqué, add ³⁄₁₆″ allowance outside dashed line. Turn under and sew on this line.

Flower & Flower reversed

Flowerpot Block Center

Leaf

Flower Center

Top of Flowerpot

For 3-D appliqué, cut on solid line. Sew on dashed line.

More patterns are on page 36.

Color photo is on page 41.

Large Quilt Assembly

1 Lay out all block patches as shown in the piecing diagram on page 36.

2 Join lettered patches to make three of each kind of block. Add appliquéd stems, leaves, bees and flowers (with regular appliqué instead of 3-D as in the small quilt). Embroider details as explained in step 6 for small quilt.

3 Lay out blocks, sashes (F) and setting squares (A) as shown in the quilt diagram. *Note:* When assembling the quilt top, press seam allowances toward the sashes. Working in rows, join three sashes and four setting squares alternately; make four rows like this. Join three blocks and four sashes alternately; make three rows like this. Join rows.

4 Sew borders to upper and lower edges of quilt top. Press seam allowances toward borders. Join KK patches to make four pinwheel corner blocks. Sew corner blocks to ends of

Cutting Requirements: Large Quilt

Finished size: 35¼" x 35¼"

Ydg.	Fabric	Use	Cut
½ yd.	Gold Print no. 1	borders	4 borders 3½" x 29"
⅛ yd.	Gold Print no. 2	flower centers, bees, sun rays	3 flower centers, 3 bees, 24 KK
½ yd.	Med. Green Print	binding, stems, leaves	binding 1½" x 4¼ yds., bias strip 1¼" x 18" for stems, 3 leaves
⅜ yd.	Light Yellow Print	sashes	24 F
⅛ yd.	Blue Print	setting squares	16 A
¼ yd.	Med. Blue Print	background, sun blocks	6 B, 3 Z, 3 Zr, 6 A, 3 AA, 3 AAr
¼ yd.	Lt. Green Print	background, watermelons	3 AA, 3 AAr, 3 E, 3 RR, 3 D, 3 KK
¼ yd.	Lt. Aqua Print	background, flowerpots	3 A, 18 KK, 3 D, 6 B, 3 AA, 3 AAr
¼ yd.	Yellow Check	sun faces, flowers, corner blocks	3 MM, 3 flowers, 16 KK
⅛ yd.*	Purple Print	bees' wings	6 bees' wings
⅛ yd.*	Med. Pink Print	flowers	6 KK
⅛ yd.	Dk. Pink Print	flowers, corner blocks	25 KK
⅛ yd.	Rust Print no. 1	tops of flowerpots	3 F
⅛ yd.	Rust Print no. 2	bottoms of flowerpots	3 FF
⅛ yd.	Dk. Green Print	watermelons	3 SS, 3 Zr, 3 KK
⅛ yd.	Red Print no. 1	watermelons, flowers	3 Zr, 3 AAr, 3 OO
⅛ yd.	Red Print no. 2	watermelons, flowers	3 Zr, 3 KK
1¼ yds.	Light Solid	lining	39" x 39"

*only a very small amount is needed: see pattern(s) for size

Also Needed: 6 ⅜" black buttons for suns' eyes, red embroidery floss for suns' mouths, black embroidery floss for watermelon seeds and bees, 39" x 39" batting

remaining two borders; sew borders to sides of quilt top.

5 Referring to the general instructions, assemble lining, batting and quilt top. Quilt in-the-ditch as shown in the quilting diagram for the small quilt. Quilt suns' rays. Add a sleeve and bind the quilt. Add buttons for eyes on the sun blocks. Or, if making a baby quilt, embroider the suns' eyes instead.

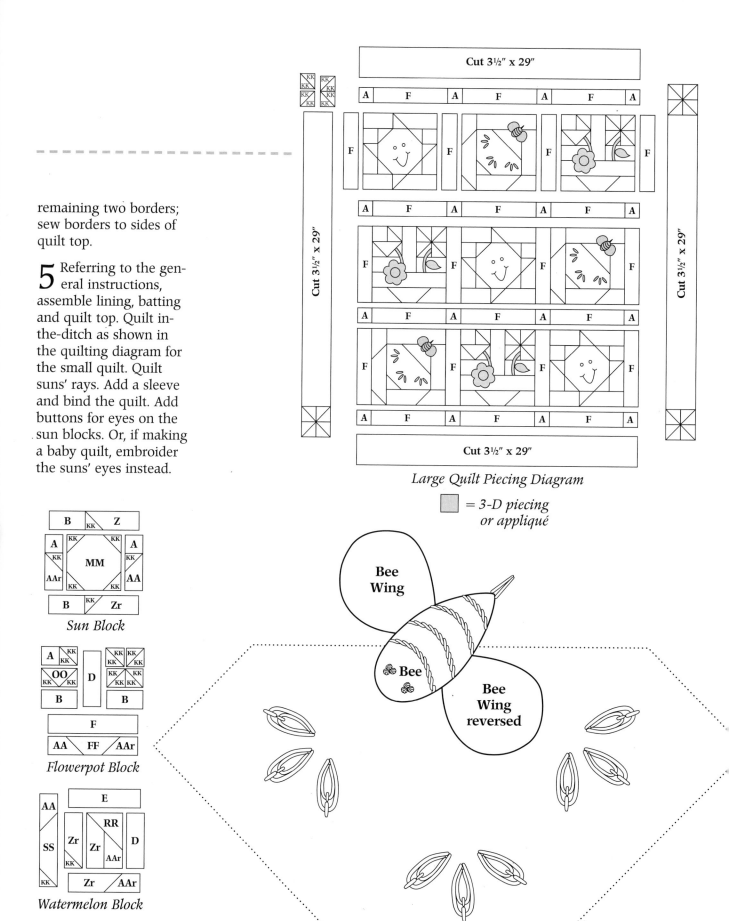

Large Quilt Piecing Diagram

= 3-D piecing or appliqué

Sun Block

Flowerpot Block

Watermelon Block

Piecing Diagram

Bring in the New (page 6)

Raggedy Ann (page 10)

Raggedy Andy (page 10)

Cupid's Arrow (page 8)

Irish Jig (page 14)

Easter Bunny (page 16)

May Basket (page 19)

I ♡ Mom (page 22)

Dear Old Dad (page 24)

Old Glory (page 28)

Summertime Picnic, small version,
(page 33)

Uncle Sam (page 26)

Star-Spangled Cats (page 29)

Detail of Summertime Picnic bee.

Cats' Meow (page 31)

Summertime Picnic, large version (page 35)

School Days, Girl (page 45)

School Days, Boy (page 45)

Detail of Girl's Face

Trick or Treat (page 49)

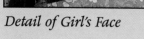

Pilgrim Boy (page 51)

Bountiful Harvest (page 54)

Pilgrim Girl (page 51)

Angels on High, small version (page 56)

Ho Ho! Oh No! (page 59)

Angels on High, large version (page 57)

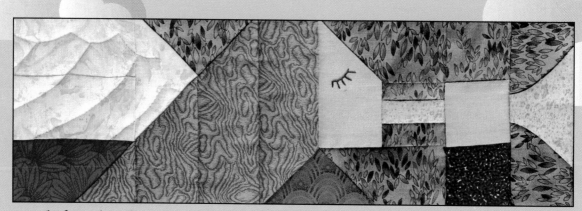

Detail of Angel Quilt

School Days

Color photos are on page 42.

School days, school days, dear old golden rule days. But are they holidays? Sure they are! Mom and Dad wouldn't argue, and many or even most kids (if they would admit it) love school. Personalize these school kids with your choices for hair, eyes, skin and clothes.

Boy Assembly

1 Lay out all patches as shown in the piecing diagram on the next page.

2 To prepare top part of hair, use fusible bonding web (following package directions) to fuse two brown print D patches with wrong sides together. Carefully (since it won't grow back) cut hair using pattern on page 47. Baste hair to green print D, matching three edges.

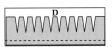

3 To prepare top part of bell tower, fold light brown A patch in half diagonally and again in half diagonally. Baste this triangle to light blue print A as shown here.

Tack top point of triangle to A patch.

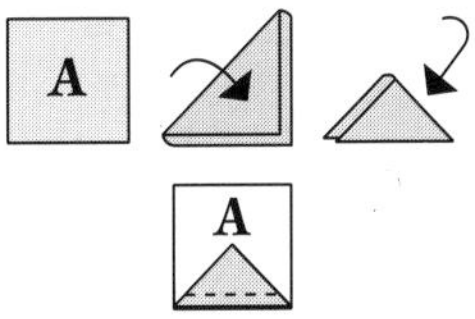

4 To prepare ears, sew two ear patches right sides together along curved edge. Turn right side out and press flat. Repeat for other ear. Baste ears to opposite

Cutting Requirements: Boy

Finished size: 11¼" x 26¼"

Ydg.	Fabric	Use	Cut
⅛ yd.	Yellow Print	borders, bell	2 K, 2 F, 1 bell
¼ yd.	Red Print	binding, border corners, school	1½" x 83", 5 A, 1 W, 1 Wr, 1 B
⅛ yd.	Light Blue Print	sky	1 NN, 1 NNr, 2 D, 1 A
⅛ yd.	Light Green Print	grass	1 U, 1 Ur, 1 D, 2 OO, 2 KK
¼ yd.	Light Peach Solid	face, ears, hands	1 MM, 4 ear patches, 2 KK
⅛ yd.	Brown Print	window, hair	1 window, 2 D, 2 KK
⅛ yd.	Light Brown Print	roof, bell tower, door	2 LL, 2 A, 1 B
¼ yd.	Blue Stripe	shirt	3 FF, 2 KK
¼ yd.	Red Print	apple	1 MM
⅛ yd.*	Green Print	leaf	2 leaves
½ yd.	Light Solid	lining	15" x 30"

*only a very small amount is needed: see pattern(s) for size

Also Needed: 2 ½" black buttons for eyes, 1 ⅜" round button for clapper on bell, 2" x 5" fusible bonding web (such as Wonder Under™), red embroidery floss for mouth, brown embroidery floss for fence and apple, 15" x 30" batting

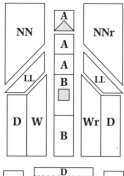

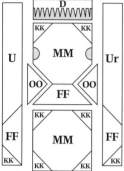

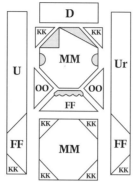

Boy Piecing Diagram   *Girl Piecing Diagram*

⬜ = *3-D piecing or appliqué*

---

sides of light peach MM as shown below.

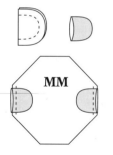

5 Join lettered patches as shown in the piecing diagram. Wherever possible, press seam allowances toward the school, apple or child. Be sure the ears are pressed away from the face.

6 Appliqué window and bell.

7 Referring to the general instructions, add border strips and corner

---

squares. Press seam allowances toward the borders.

8 To make the leaf, sew leaf patches with right sides together. Trim points. Carefully cut a small slit in one layer only. Turn leaf through slit. Press flat. Tack leaf to apple with slit side touching quilt top, using just a couple of hand stitches or a dab of glue stick. (The quilting will help secure the leaf.)

9 Use three ply floss for all embroidery. With brown floss, embroider fence in chain stitch and line on apple in outline stitch. Use brown floss to embroider apple stem in chain stitch. With red floss,

---

embroider mouth in outline stitch.

10 Referring to the general instructions, assemble lining, batting and quilt top. Quilt in-the-ditch as shown in the quilting diagram. Quilt through center of leaf. Bind the quilt. Add tabs or sleeve if desired; see page 77 for information.

11 Add buttons for eyes and clapper on bell.

Girl Assembly

1 Lay out all patches as shown in the piecing diagram.

---

2 Prepare top part of bell tower as explained in step 3 for the School Boy.

3 Prepare ears as explained in step 4 for the School Boy.

4 To make 3-D hair bangs, place brown print KK patches right sides together and sew along two short sides. Trim corner and turn right side out; press flat. Pin in place on MM and baste ⅛" from edges of patches. Sew the other part of the bangs as follows. Fold brown print C patch in half lengthwise (wrong sides together); press. Position and pin folded C strip on MM. Trim C to match shape of MM. Baste C in place, sewing ⅛" from edge.

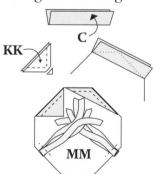

For braids, stack three brown print strips with wrong sides up. Repeat for a second stack. Baste ends of strips to MM.

7 2X8
K 2X23

A2X2
W2X67
B2X86
NN 12X67
D2X5

U2X97/8
OO 4 3/4X4 1/4
KK 2 3/4X4 3/4

Cutting Requirements: Girl

Finished size: 11¼" x 26¼"

Ydg.	Fabric	Use	Cut
⅛ yd.	Yellow Print	borders, bell	2 K, 2 F, 1 bell
¼ yd.	Red Print	binding, border corners, school	1½" x 83", 5 A, 1 W, 1 Wr, 1 B
⅛ yd.	Light Blue Print	sky	1 NN, 1 NNr, 2 D, 1 A
⅛ yd.	Light Green Print	grass	1 U, 1 Ur, 1 D, 2 OO, 4 KK
¼ yd.	Light Peach Solid	face, ears, hands	1 MM, 4 ear patches, 2 KK
⅛ yd.	Brown Print	window, hair	1 window, 2 KK, 1 C, 6 strips ½" x 8"
⅛ yd.	Light Brown Print	roof, bell tower, door	2 LL, 2 A, 1 B
⅛ yd.	Light Blue Print	shirt	3 FF, 2 KK
¼ yd.	Red Print	apple	1 MM
⅛ yd.*	Green Print	leaf	2 leaves
½ yd.	Light Solid	lining	15" x 30"

*only a very small amount is needed: see pattern(s) for size

Also Needed: 2 ½" black buttons for eyes, 1 ⅜" round button for clapper on bell, red embroidery floss for mouth, brown embroidery floss for fence and apple, 2 small gold beads for earrings, ¼ yd. of ½"-wide blue ribbon for hair ties, 15" x 30" batting

5 Baste lace to FF as shown in piecing diagram. Join lettered patches as shown in the piecing diagram. Wherever possible, press seam allowances toward the school, apple or child.

6 Appliqué window and bell.

7 Referring to the general instructions, add border strips and corner squares. Press seam allowances toward the borders.

8 Make leaf as explained in step 8 for the School Boy.

9 Do the embroidery as explained in step 9 for the School Boy.

10 Complete this step as explained in step 10 for the School Boy.

11 Add buttons for eyes and clapper on bell. Braid hair and tie ends with ribbons. If desired, sew beads to ears for earrings or use earrings of your choice.

More patterns are on the next page.

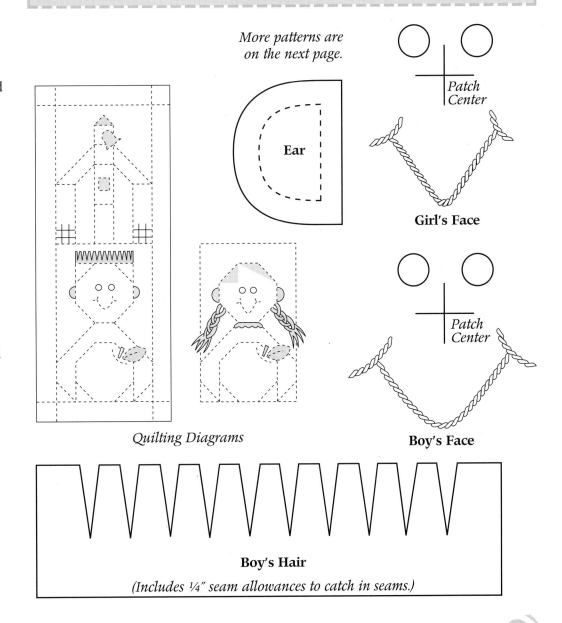

Ear

Patch Center

Girl's Face

Patch Center

Boy's Face

Quilting Diagrams

Boy's Hair

(Includes ¼" seam allowances to catch in seams.)

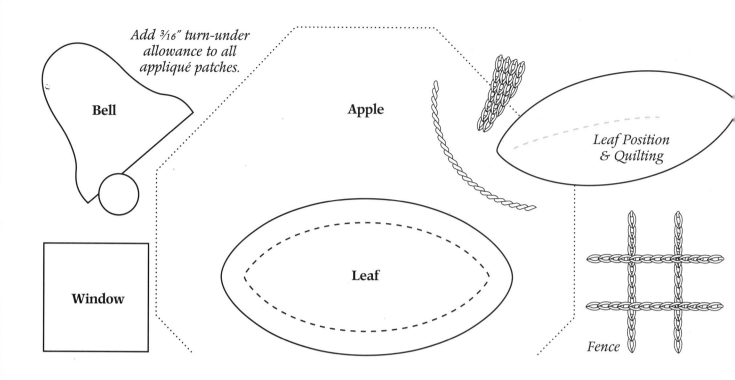

Add ³⁄₁₆″ turn-under allowance to all appliqué patches.

Bell

Apple

Leaf Position & Quilting

Window

Leaf

Fence

Make It Special–and Personal!

Use your child's school colors for the border and corner squares. Then add your child's name, a date or grade, and his or her teacher's or school's name in the apple. Use embroidery or fabric pens to add these special touches.

1 Draw lines on tracing paper ³⁄₄″ apart. Match these lines with the lines under the type and trace the letters and numbers needed. To center lines, cut apart tracing and shift left or right as needed. Tape tracing back together.

2 Tape tracing over a light source. Place apple on top and mark words in the center, allowing room for stem and leaf.

3 Using white embroidery floss, work in backstitch. A black fabric ink (permanent) will show up well if the apple is made from solid red fabric.

ABCDEFGHIJKLMN
OPQRSTUVWXYZ
abcdefghijklmn
opqrstuvwxyz
1234567890&,

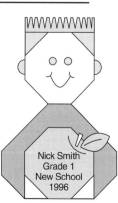

Nick Smith
Grade 1
New School
1996

Trick or Treat

Cutting Requirements

Finished size: 11¼" x 26¼"

Ydg.	Fabric	Use	Cut
⅛ yd.	Black/Tan Print	borders	2 K, 2 F
¼ yd.	Yellow/Gold Print	binding, border corners, cat's mouth	1½" x 83", 4 A, 1 cat's mouth
⅛ yd.	Black Print	background, top block	2 B, 4 KK
⅛ yd.	Blue Print	background, center block	1 FF, 2 AA, 1 OO, 1 Z
⅛ yd.	Orange Print	background, bottom block	1 OO, 2 KK, 1 Zr, 1 AA, 1 D
⅛ yd.	Orange Print	pumpkin	2 SS, 3 E
⅛ yd.*	Green Print	pumpkin stem	1 A, 1 pumpkin stem
⅛ yd.	Black Print	pumpkin eyes and mouth, cat, ghost mouth	2 pumpkin eyes, 1 pumpkin mouth, 2 KK, 1 FF, 1 AA, 1 AAr, 2 D, 2 B, 1 cat's tail, 1 ghost's mouth
⅛ yd.	White Print	ghost	1 GG, 1 GGr, 1 Z, 1 E, 1 V, 1 W
½ yd.	Light Solid	lining	15" x 30"

*only a very small amount is needed: see pattern(s) for size
Also Needed: 2 ⅜" black buttons for ghost's eyes, 2 ½" yellow buttons for cat's eyes, 15" x 30" batting

Color photo is on page 42.

Assembly

1 Lay out all patches as shown in the piecing diagram.

2 Join lettered patches as shown in the piecing diagram. Wherever possible, press seam allowances toward the pumpkin, ghost or cat. However, if dark seam allowances show through light fabric, trim dark seam allowances to be narrower than light seam allowances.

3 Appliqué pumpkin stem, eyes and mouth. Appliqué the ghost's mouth. Appliqué the cat's mouth.

4 Referring to the general instructions, add border strips and corner squares. Press seam allowances toward the borders.

5 Appliqué the cat's tail, opening the seam to tuck in the lower end of the tail. Close seam with a few hand stitches.

6 Referring to the general instructions, assemble lining, batting and quilt top. Quilt in-the-ditch as shown in the quilting diagram. Bind the quilt. Add tabs or sleeve if desired; see page 77 for information.

7 Add buttons for eyes on ghost and cat.

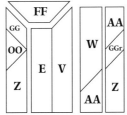
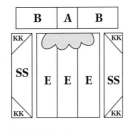
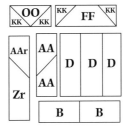

Piecing Diagram

☐ = 3-D piecing or appliqué

Boo! But don't be scared. This quilt is not too tricky, and the result is a real treat for goblins young and old. The piecing is easy and has only one set-in patch. The appliqué, too, is simple because there are no sharp points, only rounded corners.

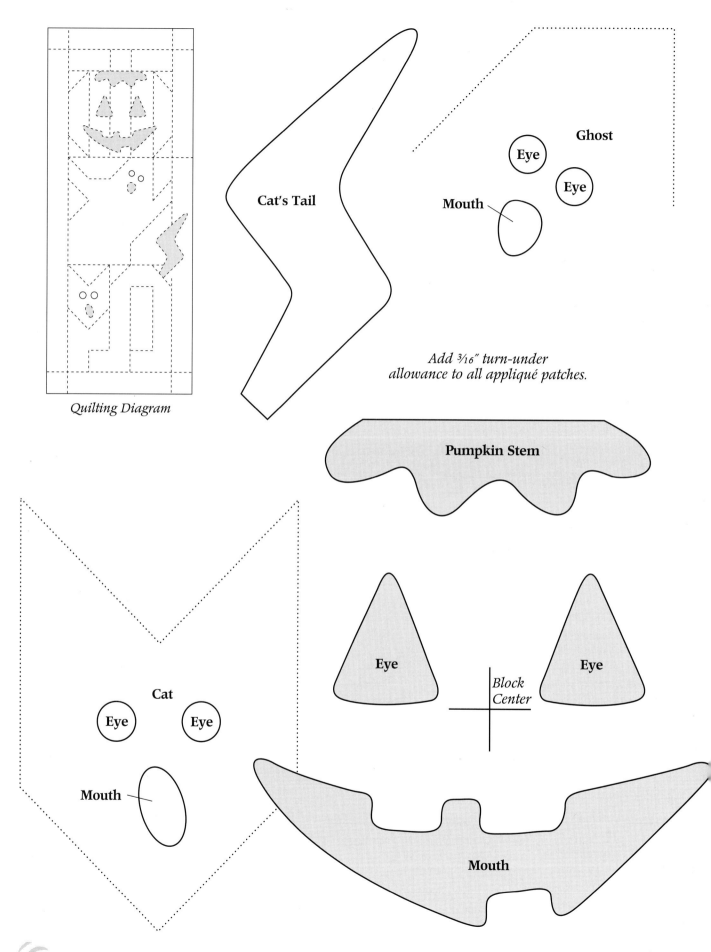

Quilting Diagram

Cat's Tail

Ghost

Eye

Eye

Mouth

*Add ³⁄₁₆″ turn-under
allowance to all appliqué patches.*

Pumpkin Stem

Eye

Eye

*Block
Center*

Cat

Eye   Eye

Mouth

Mouth

Pilgrim Pals

Color photos are on page 43.

Our young Pilgrim friends look happy to be going to a Thanksgiving feast. Even though the first such celebration happened in 1621, the smiles are the same today. For the girl's apron you could cut up an old embroidered hankie or pillowcase.

Assembly

1 **Both:** Lay out all patches as shown in the piecing diagrams on the next page.

2 **Girl:** Sew hair over face as follows. Fold rust print C patch in half lengthwise with wrong sides together. As shown below, position and pin folded C strip on peach MM. Trim C to match shape of MM. Baste hair in place, sewing 1/8" from edge.

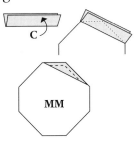

Boy: Sew hair over face as follows. Fold brown print A patch in half diagonally with wrong sides together and press. Position A so that the square corners of the triangle and the corner of peach S match; pin in place. Repeat for other brown print A patch. Baste A triangles in place, sewing 1/8" from the edge.

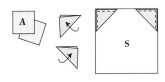

3 **Girl:** Sew hands (KKs) to pie pan (FF). Position piecrust edge on long edge of blue/white FF, matching straight edges. Turn under and blindstitch the curved

Cutting Requirements: Pilgrim Girl

Finished size: 11¼" x 26¼"

Ydg.	Fabric	Use	Cut
1/8 yd.	Brown Print	borders	2 K, 2 F
1/4 yd.	Gold Print	binding, border corners	1½" x 83", 4 A
1/8 yd.	Light Teal Print	background	1 F, 2 RR, 2 OO, 4 KK
1/4 yd.	Lt. Peach Solid	face, hands	1 MM, 2 KK
1/8 yd.*	Med. Peach Solid	cheeks	2 cheeks
1/8 yd.	Rust Print	hair	1 C, 2 OO
1/8 yd.	White Print	cap, collar, apron	1 FF, 2 KK, 2 OO, 1 GG, 1 GGr, 1 apron cut 7¼" x 5"
1/8 yd.	Black Print	sleeves, skirt	2 B, 1 U, 1 Ur, 3 I
1/8 yd.	Black Print	dress	1 FF, 1 D, 2 KK, 2 A
1/8 yd.*	Tan Print	piecrust	1 FF, 1 piecrust edge
1/8 yd.*	Blue/White Print	pie pan	1 FF
1/2 yd.	Light Solid	lining	15" x 30"

*only a very small amount is needed: see pattern(s) for size

Also Needed: 7¼" of ½"-wide white eyelet lace for apron, 10" of ¼"-wide white ribbon for bow, 2 ½" black buttons for eyes, red embroidery floss for mouth, white embroidery floss for steam, dark brown embroidery floss for holes in piecrust, green and orange embroidery floss for apron, 15" x 30" batting

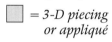

Pilgrim Girl

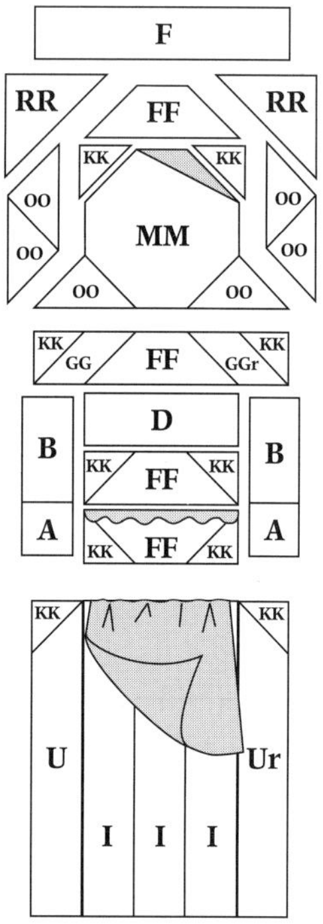

F

RR	FF	RR
KK		KK
OO		OO
OO	MM	OO
OO	OO	

KK	GG	FF	GGr	KK
B	KK	D	KK	B
A	KK	FF	KK	A

KK		KK
U		Ur
I	I	I

Piecing Diagram

☐ = 3-D piecing or appliqué

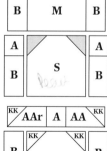

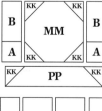

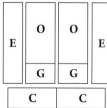

Pilgrim Boy

B	M	B
A		A
B	S	B

KK	AAr	A	AA	KK
B	KK	MM	KK	B
A	KK		KK	A
KK	PP	KK

E	O	O	E
	G	G	
C	C

Piecing Diagram

☐ = 3-D piecing or appliqué

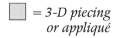

Cutting Requirements: Pilgrim Boy

Finished size: 11¼" x 26¼"

Ydg.	Fabric	Use	Cut
⅛ yd.	Brown Print	borders	2 K, 2 F
¼ yd.	Gold Print	binding, border corners	1½" x 83", 4 A
⅛ yd.	Light Teal Print	background	4 B, 4 KK, 2 E
¼ yd.	Light Peach Solid	face, hands	1 S, 2 KK
⅛ yd.*	Brown Print	hair	2 A
⅛ yd.	Black Solid	hat, sleeves, boots, buckle centers	1 M, 4 A, 2 B, 2 G, 2 C, 1 hat buckle center, 2 shoe buckle centers
⅛ yd.*	Gold Print	buckles	1 hat buckle, 2 shoe buckles
⅛ yd.*	White Print	collar	1 AA, 1 AAr
⅛ yd.	Black Print	shirt	1 A, 2 KK, 1 PP
⅛ yd.*	Green Solid	pumpkin stem	1 pumpkin stem
¼ yd.	Orange Solid	pumpkin	1 MM
⅛ yd.	Brown Solid	pants	2 O
½ yd.	Light Solid	lining	15" x 30"

*only a very small amount is needed: see pattern(s) for size
Also Needed: 2 ½" black buttons for eyes, red embroidery floss for mouth, 15" x 30" batting

edge of the piecrust. The straight edge will be caught in the seam when patches are joined.

4 Girl: Make apron as follows. To hem the apron, fold over bottom (long) edge ¼" and press. Fold over another ¼" and press again. Pin eyelet lace to underside of hem and sew through all layers. Finish sides of apron by folding over ¼", another ¼", and sewing. Using two ply of green floss, embroider vine and pumpkin stem in backstitch and leaves with single lazy daisy stitches. Using two ply of orange floss, embroider pumpkin in backstitch. Gather top edge of apron by sewing ⅛" from edge with a long stitch (4-6 stitches per inch). Pull thread so that top edge measures about 4½". The gathers can be adjusted when the apron is pinned in place.

5 Both: Join lettered patches as shown in the piecing diagrams.

Girl: After assembling the lower (skirt) section, pin apron in place over I patches so the gathered edge will be caught in the seam. Adjust gathers to fit. Finish joining the patches.

Both: Wherever possible, press seam allowances toward the Pilgrim.

6 Girl: Appliqué the cheeks.

Boy: Appliqué the pumpkin stem at the top of the pumpkin. Appliqué gold buckle patches on shoes and hat, then appliqué black buckle center patches over gold buckles.

7 Both: Use three ply floss for all remaining embroidery. Using red floss, embroider the mouths in outline stitch.

Girl: Using white floss,

embroider steam (above pie) in backstitch. Using dark brown floss, embroider holes in piecrust in lazy daisy stitch.

8 Both: Referring to the general instructions, add border strips and corner squares. Press seam allowances toward the borders.

9 Both: Referring to the general instructions, assemble lining, batting and quilt top. Quilt in-the-ditch as shown in the quilting diagrams.

Boy: Quilt the pumpkin as shown at right.

Both: Bind the quilt. Add tabs or sleeve if desired; see page 77 for information.

10 Girl: Tie ribbon to make a bow and sew it to the quilt.

Both: Sew on buttons for eyes.

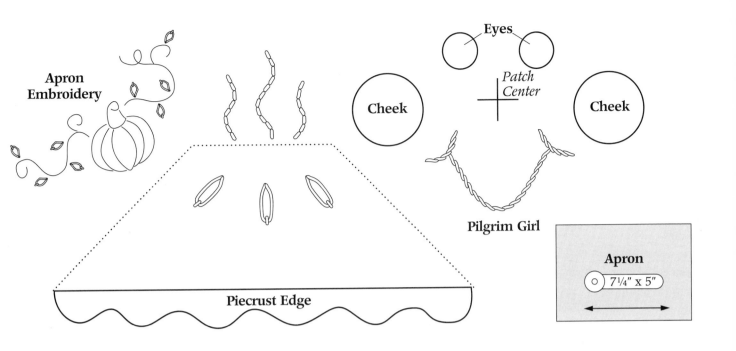

Apron Embroidery

Eyes

Cheek Patch Center Cheek

Pilgrim Girl

Piecrust Edge

Apron
⊙ 7¼" x 5"

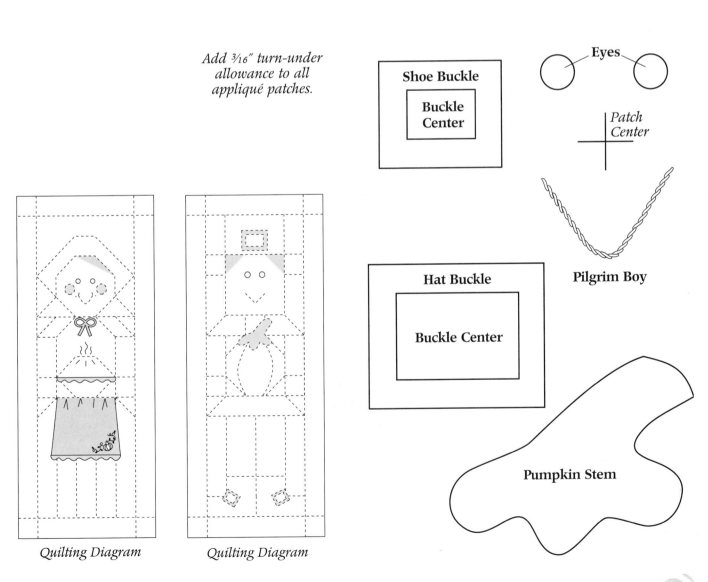

Add ³⁄₁₆" turn-under allowance to all appliqué patches.

Shoe Buckle

Buckle Center

Eyes

Patch Center

Pilgrim Boy

Hat Buckle

Buckle Center

Pumpkin Stem

Quilting Diagram   *Quilting Diagram*

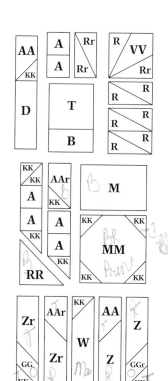

Color photo on page 43.

Autumn's bounty yields a wonderful harvest–just don't say that to the turkey! Celebrate the season with this festive quilt that might very well take less time to make than Thanksgiving dinner.

Bountiful Harvest

Assembly

1 Lay out all patches as shown in the piecing diagram.

2 Join lettered patches as shown in the piecing diagram to make the three blocks. Sew blocks together. Wherever possible, press seam allowances toward the turkey, cornucopia or leaf.

3 Appliqué the turkey's wattle and the leaf stem, opening seams as necessary to tuck in ends. Close seams.

4 Use three ply floss for all embroidery. With black floss, make three small french knots for the turkey's eye. Using gold floss, make turkey's legs with double rows of chain stitch.

5 Referring to the general instructions, add border strips and corner squares. Press seam allowances toward the borders.

6 Appliqué fruit in cornucopia, working in numerical order. With gold floss, embroider apple stem (fruit no. 2) and "shine" on fruit no. 5 in satin stitch.

7 Referring to the general instructions, assemble lining, batting and quilt top. Quilt in-the-ditch as shown in the quilting diagram. Bind the quilt. Add tabs or sleeve if desired; see page 77 for information.

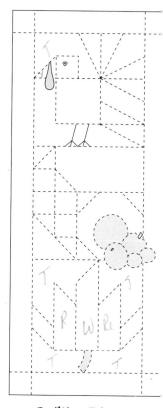

Quilting Diagram

Piecing Diagram

■ = *3-D piecing or appliqué*

Cutting Requirements

Finished size: 11¼" x 26¼"

Ydg.	Fabric	Use	Cut
⅛ yd.	Gold Print	borders	2 K, 2 F
¼ yd.	Brown Print	binding, border corners, inside of cornucopia	1½" x 83", 4 A, 1 MM
⅛ yd.	Light Teal Print	background	2 AA, 1 AAr, 1 A, 1 R, 1 Rr, 1 D, 1 B, 1 Z, 1 Zr, 3 KK, 1 F
⅛ yd.	Blue Print	background	3 KK, 1 AAr, 1 M, 1 RR
⅛ yd.*	Rust Print	turkey's head and body	1 A, 1 T
⅛ yd.*	Dark Yellow Print	turkey's beak	1 KK
⅛ yd.	Red Solid	turkey feathers, fruit, leaf	2 R, 1 Rr, 1 VV, 1 fruit no. 5, 1 Z, 1 Zr
⅛ yd.	Maroon Print	turkey feathers, wattle, fruit, leaf	3 R, 1 wattle, 1 fruit no. 4, 1 W
⅛ yd.	Orange Solid	turkey feathers, fruit, leaf	1 R, 1 Rr, 1 each fruit no. 1 and no. 3, 1 GG, 1 GGr, 1 stem
⅛ yd.	Gold Print	cornucopia	4 KK, 2 A
⅛ yd.	Light Brown Print	cornucopia	2 A, 2 KK
⅛ yd.*	Green Solid	fruit	1 fruit no. 2
½ yd.	Light Solid	lining	15" x 30"

*only a very small amount is needed: see pattern(s) for size

Also Needed: black embroidery floss for turkey's eye, gold embroidery floss for turkey's legs and fruit, 15" x 30" batting

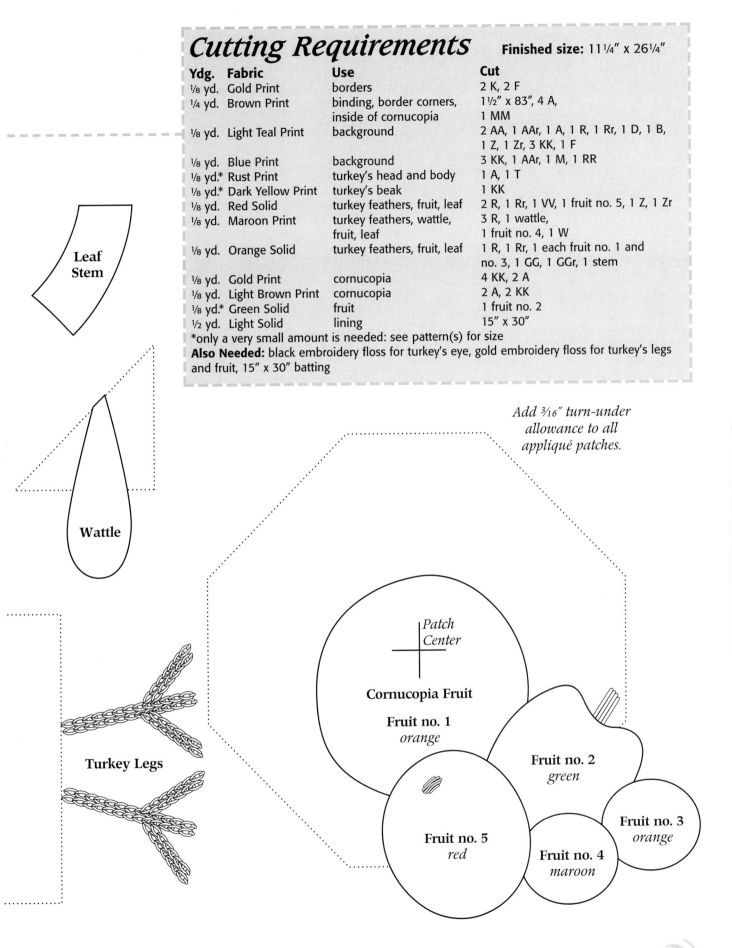

Add ³⁄₁₆" turn-under allowance to all appliqué patches.

Leaf Stem

Wattle

Turkey Legs

Patch Center

Cornucopia Fruit

Fruit no. 1
orange

Fruit no. 2
green

Fruit no. 3
orange

Fruit no. 5
red

Fruit no. 4
maroon

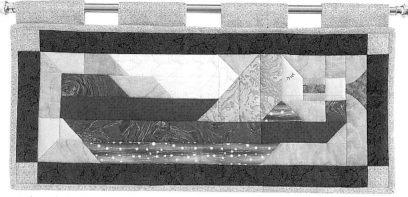

Angels on High

Color photo is on page 43.

These angels are blowing their golden trumpets to announce the good news of Christmas. Whether you make the small quilt or the larger one, you will find the sewing easy with only a few set-in patches, a little hand appliqué and just a touch of simple embroidery.

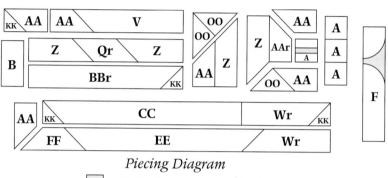

Piecing Diagram

☐ = *3-D piecing or appliqué*

Small Quilt Assembly

1 Lay out all patches as shown in the piecing diagram.

2 Join lettered patches as shown in the piecing diagram. Wherever possible, press seam allowances toward the angel. If necessary, trim dark seam allowances to prevent them from showing through the light fabrics.

3 Appliqué the two patches for the trumpet, opening seams as necessary to tuck in edges of appliqué patches. Close seams. The long, straight edge of the trumpet will be caught in the seam when borders are added.

4 Using two ply of green floss, embroider eye in buttonhole stitch. Weave in the ends so they don't show.

5 Referring to the general instructions, add border strips and corner squares. Press seam allowances toward the borders.

6 Referring to the general instructions, assemble lining, batting and quilt top. Quilt in-the-ditch as shown in the quilting diagram. Quilt wing as shown on page 58. Bind the quilt. Add tabs or sleeve if desired; see page 77 for information.

Cutting Requirements: Small Quilt

Finished Size: 26¼" x 11¼"

Ydg.	Fabric	Use	Cut
⅛ yd.	Purple Print	borders	2 K, 2 F
¼ yd.	Yellow/Gold Print	binding, border corners	1½" x 83", 4 A
⅛ yd.	Light Teal Print	background	2 KK, 3 AA, 1 OO, 2 A, 1 F, 1 B, 1 Qr, 1 FF, 1 Wr
⅛ yd.	Light Peach Solid	feet, face, hand	2 AA, 1 KK, 1 AAr, 1 A
⅛ yd.	White Print	wing	1 V, 1 Z, 1 OO
⅛ yd.	Light Gold Print	hair	1 KK, 1 AA, 2 Z
⅛ yd.*	Dark Gold Print	trumpet	1 each piece of trumpet
⅛ yd.	Dark Red Print	robe	1 BBr, 1 Wr
⅛ yd.	Med. Red Print	robe	1 Z, 1 CC, 1 A
⅛ yd.	Light Red Print	robe	1 OO, 1 EE
½ yd.	Light Solid	lining	30" x 15"

*only a very small amount is needed: see pattern(s) for size

Also Needed: green embroidery floss for eye, 30" x 15" batting

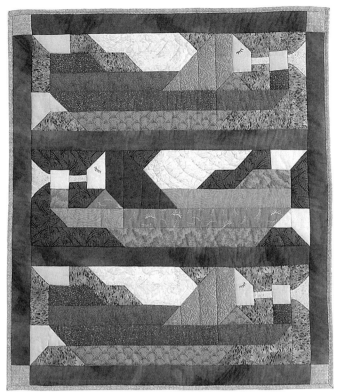

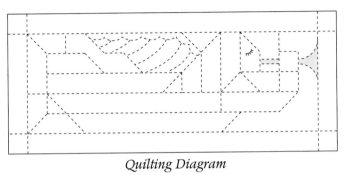

Quilting Diagram

Color photo is on page 44.

Large Quilt Assembly

Appliqué and quilting patterns for Angels on High are on the next page.

1 Lay out all patches as shown in the piecing diagrams on pages 56 (top and bottom panel) and 58 (center panel).

2 Join lettered patches to make the three panels. Two of the panels are identical, whereas the center panel uses different colors and the angel is facing to the left instead of to the right. Therefore, asymmetrical patches are reversed. Wherever possible, press seam allowances toward the angels. If necessary, trim dark seam allowances to prevent them from showing through the light fabrics.

Cutting Requirements: Large Quilt

Finished size: 26¼" x 29¼"

Ydg.	Fabric	Use	Cut
³⁄₈ yd.	Purple Print	borders/sashes	2 borders 2" x 26", 4 borders/sashes 2" x 23" (same as K)
¼ yd.	Light Gold Print	binding, border corners	1½" x 3¼ yds., 4 A
¼ yd.	Teal Print	background, two blocks	4 KK, 6 AA, 2 OO, 4 A, 2 F, 2 B, 2 Qr, 2 FF, 2 Wr
⅛ yd.	Blue Print	background, center block	2 KK, 3 AAr, 1 OO, 2 A, 1 F, 1 B, 1 Q, 1 FF, 1 W
⅛ yd.	Peach Solid	feet, faces, hands, two bks.	4 AA, 2 KK, 2 AAr, 2 A
⅛ yd.	Lt. Pink Solid	feet, face, hand, center bk.	2 AAr, 1 KK, 1 AA, 1 A
⅛ yd.	Off-White Print	wings, two blocks	2 V, 2 Z, 2 OO
⅛ yd.	Lt. Gray Print	wing, center block	1 Vr, 1 Zr, 1 OO
⅛ yd.	Light Brown Print	hair, two blocks	2 KK, 2 AA, 4 Z
⅛ yd.	Med. Brown Print	hair, center block	1 KK, 1 AAr, 2 Zr
⅛ yd.	Pink Print no. 1	robes, two blocks	2 Z, 2 A, 2 CC
⅛ yd.	Pink Print no. 2	robes, two blocks	2 BBr, 2 Wr
⅛ yd.	Pink Print no. 3	robes, two blocks	2 OO, 2 EE
⅛ yd.	Gold Print no. 1	robe, center block	1 Zr, 1 A, 1 EE
⅛ yd.	Gold Print no. 2	robe, center block	1 BB, 1 W
⅛ yd.	Gold Print no. 3	robe, center block	1 OO, 1 CCr
⅛ yd.	Yellow Print	trumpets	3 each piece of trumpet
1 yd.	Light Solid	lining	30" x 33"

Also Needed: green embroidery floss for eyes, 30" x 33" batting

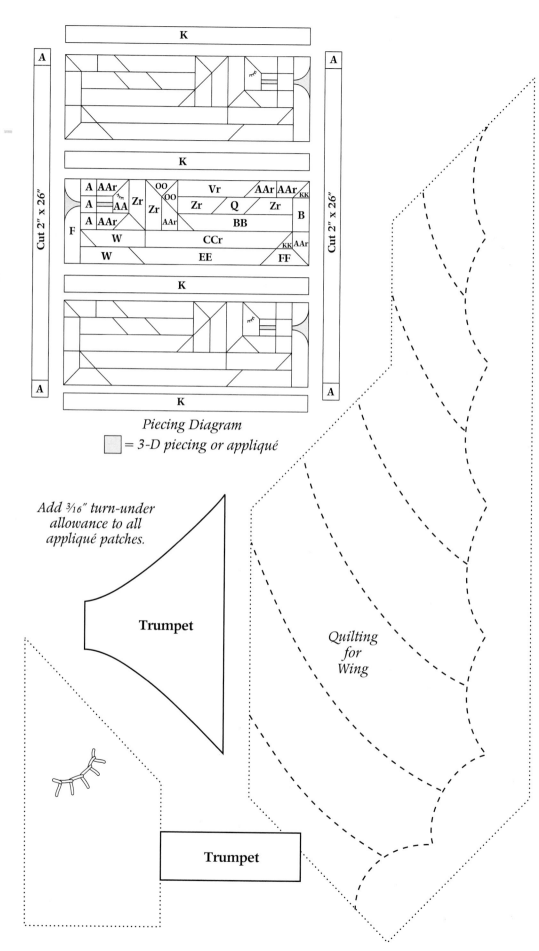

3 For each of the panels, appliqué the two patches for the trumpet, opening seams as necessary to tuck in edges of appliqué patches. Close seams. The long, straight edges of the trumpets will be caught in the seams when borders are added.

4 Using two ply of green floss, embroider eyes in buttonhole stitch.

5 Join panels with purple print sashes (Ks) between them. Referring to the general instructions, add border strips and corner squares. Press seam allowances toward the sashes and borders.

6 Referring to the general instructions, assemble lining, batting and quilt top. Quilt in-the-ditch as shown in the quilting diagram for the small quilt. Quilt wings as shown at right, reversing the wing quilting motif for the center panel. Bind the quilt. Add tabs or sleeve if desired; see page 77 for information.

Piecing Diagram

☐ = 3-D piecing or appliqué

Add 3/16" turn-under allowance to all appliqué patches.

Trumpet

Trumpet

Quilting for Wing

Ho Ho! Oh No!

Assembly

1 Lay out all patches as shown in the piecing diagram.

2 To make ears, sew two patches (with right sides together) along curved edge. Turn right side out and press flat. Repeat for other ear. Baste ears to short sides of M patch as shown here.

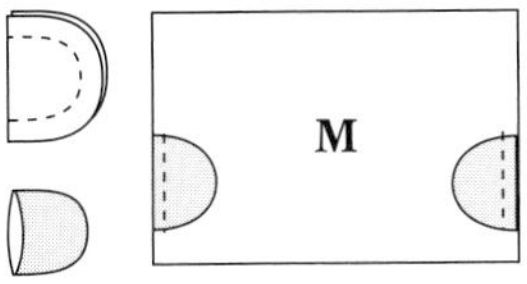

3 To make mittens, sew mitten and mitten reversed with right sides together along curved edges. Clip at indentation. Turn right side out and press flat.

Repeat for other mitten. Baste mittens to white/black F patch, placing outer edges ¼" from ends of F to allow for seams.

4 Join lettered patches as shown in the piec-

ing diagram on the next page. Before joining the two M patches, pin or baste the felt beard to the upper edge of the white M so that it will be caught in the seam. Wherever possible, press seam allowances toward Santa or the chimney.

5 To make the mustache, sew mustache patch and a reversed patch (right sides together) around long edges. Trim point and turn right side out. Press flat. Repeat for other mustache patches. Tack

Color photo is on page 44.

Don't worry, Santa, you aren't really stuck! Just pull in your tummy and you will be on your merry way. Quilters, too, will be on their merry way with this jolly quilt that incorporates three-dimensional piecing and simple appliqué. Find hints for making 3-D patches on page 21.

Cutting Requirements

Finished size: 11¼" x 26¼"

Ydg.	Fabric	Use	Cut
⅛ yd.	Green Print	borders	2 K, 2 F
¼ yd.	Red Print	binding, border corners, chimney	1½" x 83", 10 A
⅛ yd.	Light Blue Print	background	1 DDr, 1 KK, 3 I, 1 F, 1 R, 1 Rr
⅛ yd.	Peach Solid	face, ears	1 M, 4 ears
⅛ yd.	White Felt or 1 square	beard	1 beard
⅛ yd.	White Print	hat, underneath beard	1 D, 1 pompom, 1 M
⅛ yd.*	Pink Solid	nose	1 nose
⅛ yd.*	Red Solid	mouth	1 mouth
⅛ yd.	White/Blue Print	eyebrows, mustache	1 eyebrow & 1 reversed, 2 mustache patches & 2 reversed
⅛ yd.	Light Red Print	hat, shirt	1 QQ, 1 UU
⅛ yd.	Med. Red Print	chimney	3 B
⅛ yd.	Dark Red Print	chimney	3 B
⅛ yd.	Light Green Print	mittens	2 mittens & 2 mittens reversed
⅛ yd.	Dark Green Print	holly leaves	2 holly leaves & 2 reversed
⅛ yd.	White/Black Print	chimney top	1 F
½ yd.	Light Solid	lining	15" x 30"

*only a very small amount is needed: see pattern(s) for size

Also Needed: 2 ⅝" blue buttons for eyes, 3 ⅝" red buttons for holly berries, 15" x 30" batting

patches together as shown here. Baste mustache on face M.

Appliqué pink nose (with a circle of batting underneath if you want extra puffiness) over mustache, sewing through all layers. Appliqué mouth to beard, sewing only through the beard. Appliqué eyebrows.

6 Referring to the general instructions, add border strips and corner squares. Press seam allowances toward the borders.

7 Appliqué pompom, which will overlap the border.

8 Referring to the general instructions, assemble lining, batting and quilt top. Quilt in-the-ditch as shown in the quilting diagram. Be sure to lift up the beard before quilting around the M patch underneath. Quilt two lines through Santa's jacket (UU). Bind the quilt. Add tabs or sleeve if desired; see page 77 for information.

9 Make holly leaves by sewing leaf and leaf reversed (right sides together) around all sides. Trim points and clip inner curves. Carefully cut a small slit in one layer; turn leaf through the slit. Press flat. Repeat for other leaf. Tack leaves to quilt. Add red buttons for holly berries. Add blue buttons for eyes.

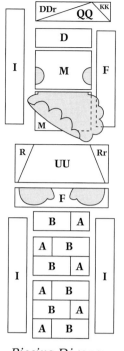

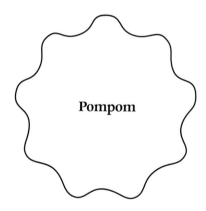

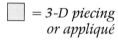

Piecing Diagram

= 3-D piecing
or appliqué

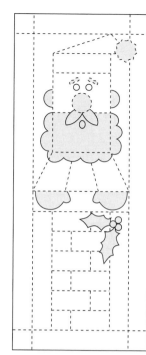

Quilting Diagram

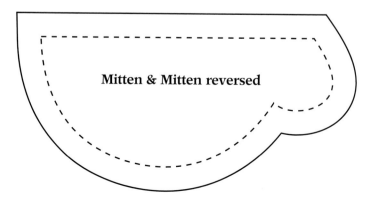

Pompom

**Mustache &
Mustache reversed**

Mitten & Mitten reversed

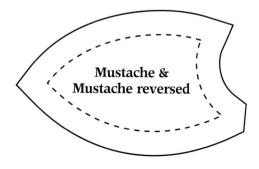

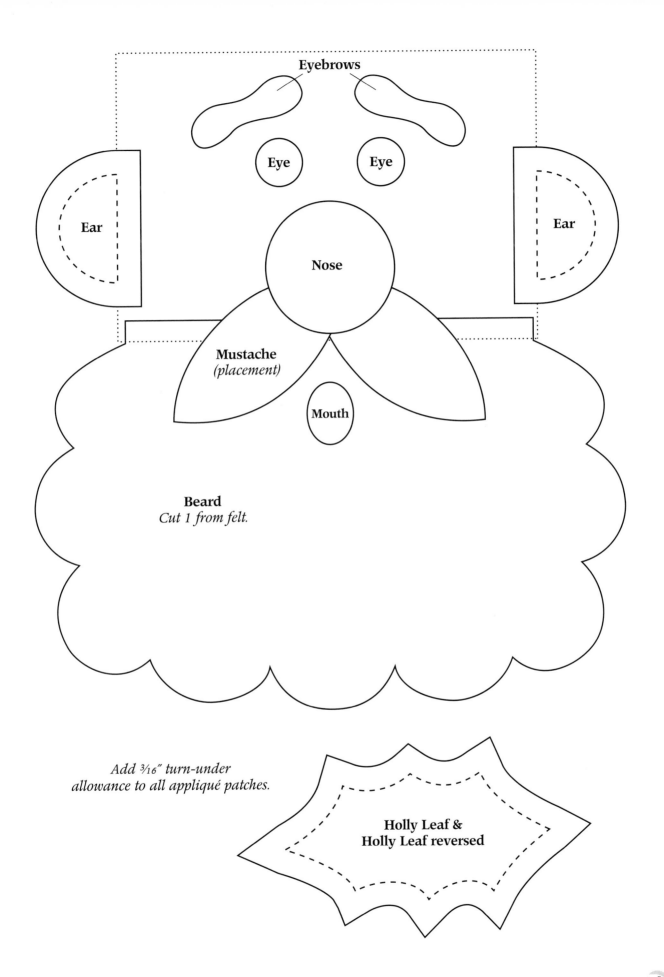

Eyebrows

Eye   Eye

Ear   Ear

Nose

Mustache
(placement)

Mouth

Beard
Cut 1 from felt.

Add ³⁄₁₆″ turn-under
allowance to all appliqué patches.

Holly Leaf &
Holly Leaf reversed

Rotary Cutting Tips

1 All of the pattern pieces in this section can be cut with a rotary cutter instead of scissors. Be sure to use a cutting mat to protect your work surface, and use a sharp blade in the rotary cutter. If you have to use scissors to cut spots the blade missed, it's time for a new blade. For safety's sake, keep the guard on when not actually cutting. It is helpful to have a variety of cutting rulers, but if you have only one, it should be 6″ x 24″ so you can cut strips across the fabric width.

2 The yardage amounts needed for these quilts are small. However, if you need to cut off a significant amount to square up the fabric or if you make a mistake, it is possible you might need a little more yardage than called for. Always cut the largest pieces first. Many of the cutting dimensions show triangles that are cut away and not used, and this causes some waste.

3 Square up your fabric before cutting strips or patches. To do this,

accurately place a 24″ ruler perpendicular to the fold. Cut off the minimum necessary to square the fabric.

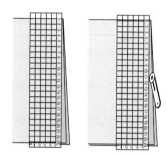

4 All but six of the patterns can be cut from strips, rectangles or squares by using the dimensions given inside the patterns. All dimensions include seam allowances, so you can simply use a cutting ruler instead of individual patterns, especially for rec-

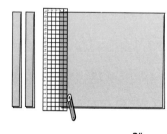

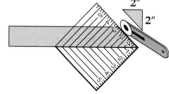

tangles and squares. However, for patterns with angles other than square corners, it is a good idea to first cut strips or rectangles, cut away the "waste" triangles (shown in white on the diagrams) and then use the pattern to trim the points. To do this, place the pattern on the cut strip and use scissors or a small ruler and the cutter to trim points. Trimmed points will make construction very easy and accurate because there is no doubt about how the patches fit together.

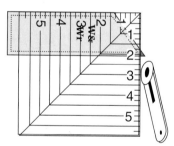

5 For the patterns that do not have cutting dimensions (because they cannot be rotary cut easily and accurately using common ruler measurements), trace or photocopy (check for accuracy!)

the pattern and cut it out on the solid line. Place the pattern on the fabric and use a small ruler (for ease in handling) to cut accurately around the pattern.

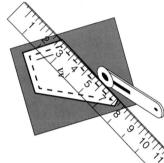

6 For patches that are reversed (noted with an "r" in the cutting requirements), place pattern face down on fabric before cutting. When you need both a shape and its reverse (such as AA & AAr), place fabric strips wrong sides together before cutting.

7 If your pattern scoots around while cutting, put a small piece of double-stick tape on it to hold it securely on the top layer of fabric. To keep the ruler from slipping, cut small (¼″) pieces of sandpaper and use super glue to fasten them to the underside of the ruler.

Patterns appear in
alphabetical order
and tend to be
grouped by shape.

*Align arrows with lengthwise
or crosswise grain of fabric.*

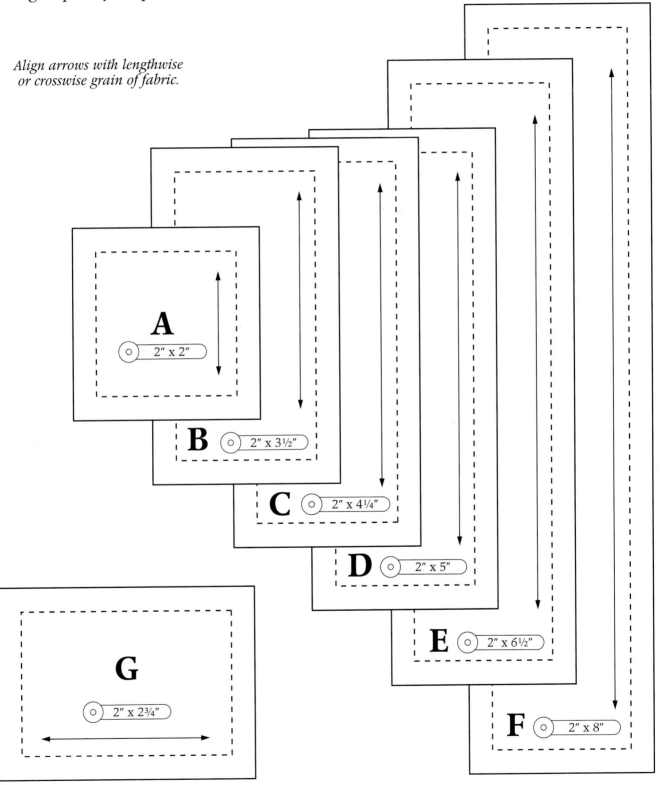

A ⊙—— 2" x 2"

B ⊙—— 2" x 3½"

C ⊙—— 2" x 4¼"

D ⊙—— 2" x 5"

E ⊙—— 2" x 6½"

F ⊙—— 2" x 8"

G ⊙—— 2" x 2¾"

Patterns H-K

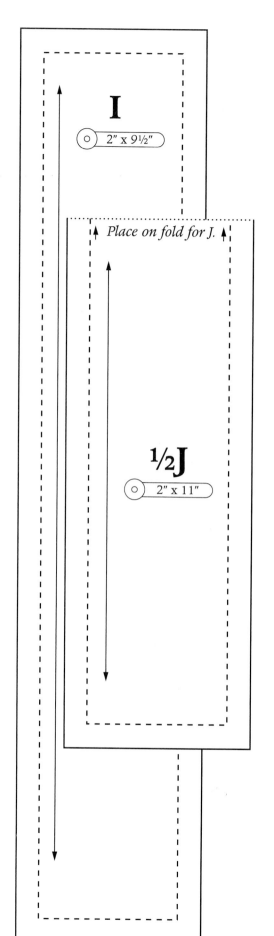

I

◉ 2" x 9½"

Place on fold for J.

½J

◉ 2" x 11"

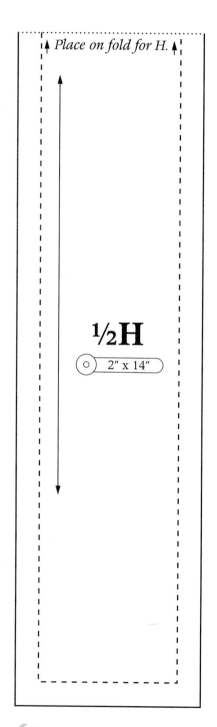

Place on fold for H.

½H

◉ 2" x 14"

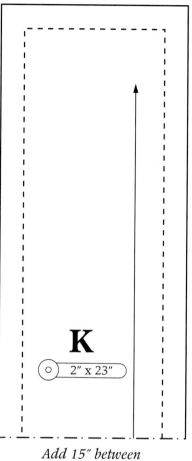

K

◉ 2" x 23"

Add 15" between dot/dash lines.

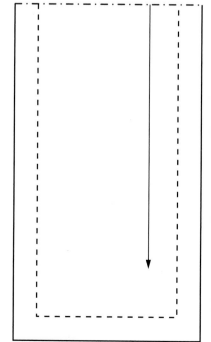

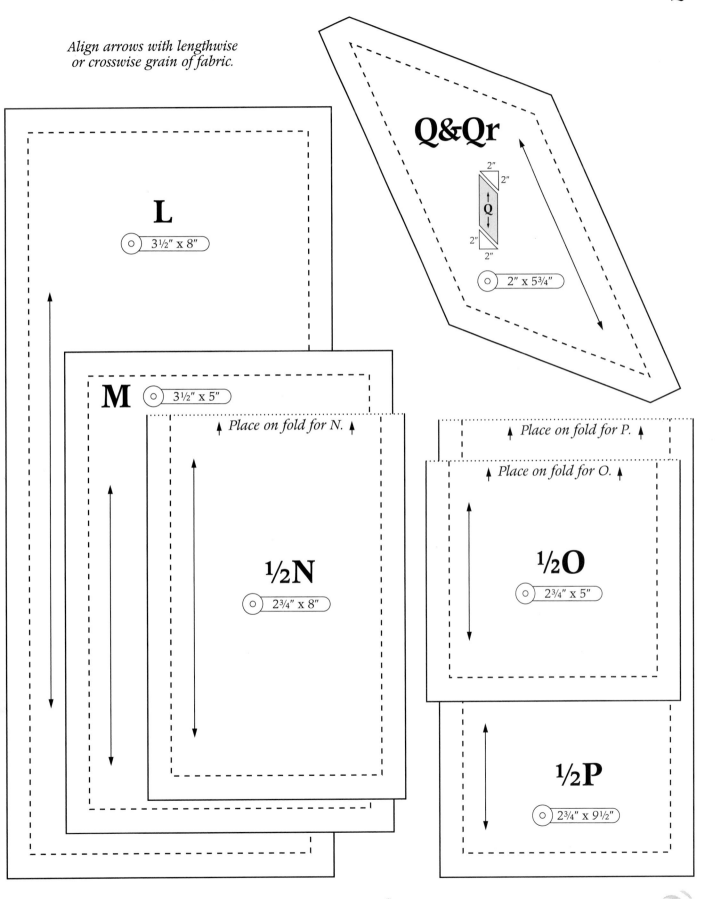

Align arrows with lengthwise
or crosswise grain of fabric.

Q&Qr

2"
2"

Q

2"
2"

○ 2" x 5¾"

L

○ 3½" x 8"

M ○ 3½" x 5"

▲ *Place on fold for N.* ▲

½N

○ 2¾" x 8"

▲ *Place on fold for P.* ▲

▲ *Place on fold for O.* ▲

½O

○ 2¾" x 5"

½P

○ 2¾" x 9½"

Patterns R-V

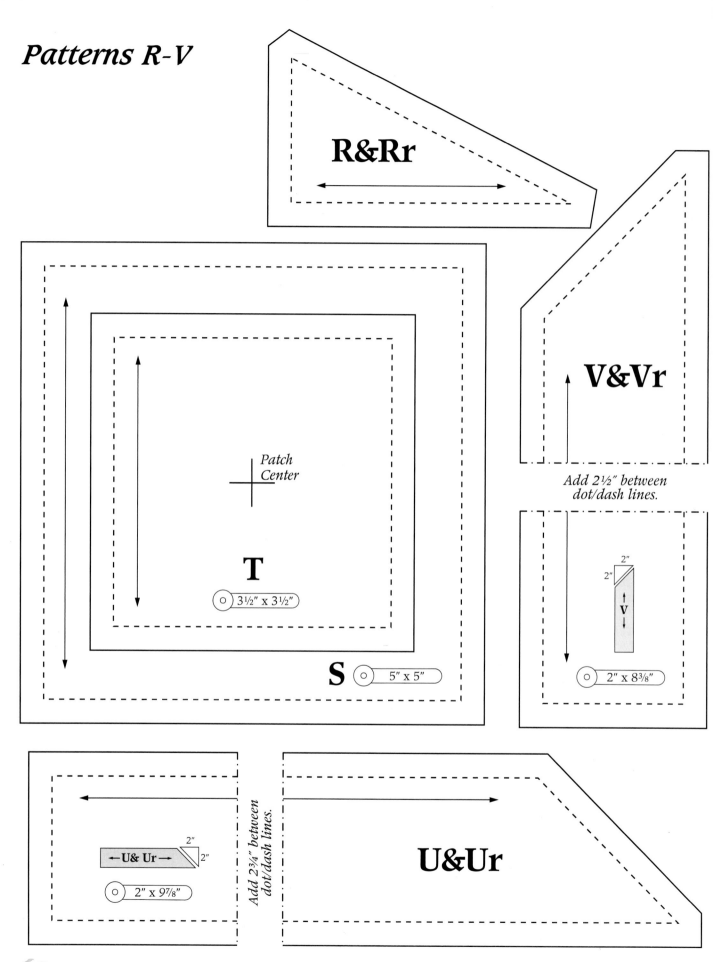

R&Rr

V&Vr

Patch Center

T

⊙ 3½" x 3½"

S ⊙ 5" x 5"

Add 2½" between dot/dash lines.

2"

2"

V

⊙ 2" x 8⅜"

2"

←U& Ur→ 2"

⊙ 2" x 9⅞"

Add 2¾" between dot/dash lines.

U&Ur

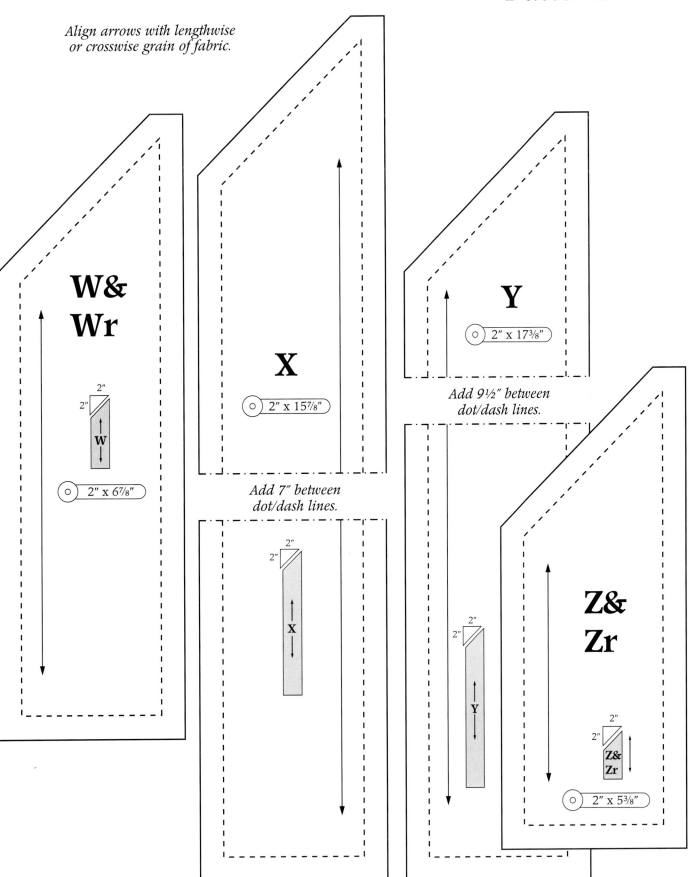

Align arrows with lengthwise or crosswise grain of fabric.

W& Wr

2"
2"
W
2" x 6⁷⁄₈"

X

2" x 15⁷⁄₈"

Add 7" between dot/dash lines.

2"
2"
X

Y

2" x 17³⁄₈"

Add 9½" between dot/dash lines.

2"
2"
Y

Z& Zr

2"
2"
Z& Zr
2" x 5³⁄₈"

Patterns AA-EE

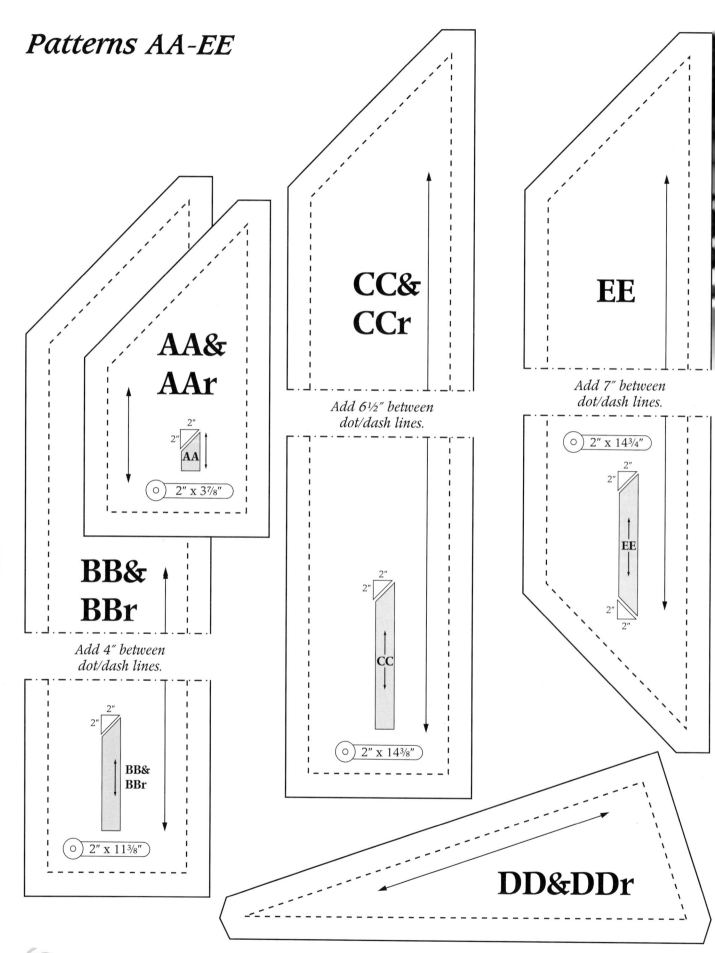

AA&
AAr

2"
2"
AA

2" x 3⅞"

BB&
BBr

Add 4" between
dot/dash lines.

2"
2"
BB&
BBr

2" x 11⅜"

CC&
CCr

Add 6½" between
dot/dash lines.

2"
2"
CC

2" x 14⅜"

EE

Add 7" between
dot/dash lines.

2" x 14¾"

2"
2"
EE
2"
2"

DD&DDr

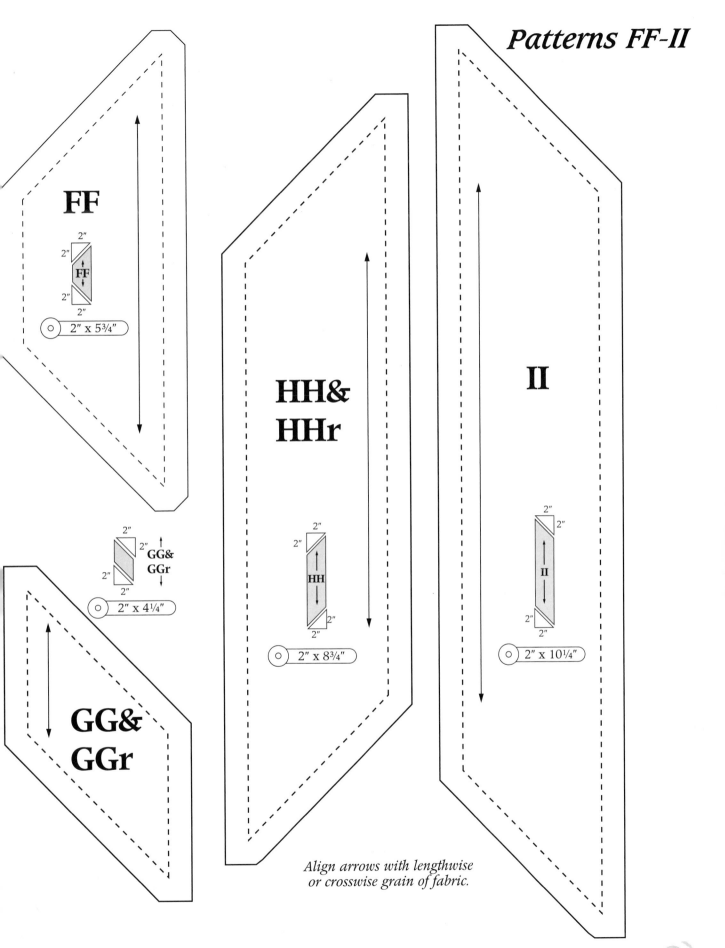

FF

2"
2"
FF
2"
2"

2" x 5¾"

GG& GGr

2"
2" GG& GGr
2"
2"

2" x 4¼"

HH& HHr

2"
2"
HH
2"
2"

2" x 8¾"

II

2"
2"
II
2"
2"

2" x 10¼"

Align arrows with lengthwise or crosswise grain of fabric.

Patterns JJ-MM

*Align arrows with lengthwise
or crosswise grain of fabric.*

KK

KK
KK
2³⁄₈" x 2³⁄₈"

LL

1⁵⁄₈"
1⁵⁄₈"
LL
LL
1⁵⁄₈"
1⁵⁄₈"
3⁷⁄₈" x 3⁷⁄₈"

**JJ&
JJr**

2"
2"
JJ&
JJr
2"
2"
2" x 7¹⁄₄"

MM

*Patch
Center*

1⁵⁄₈"   1⁵⁄₈"
1⁵⁄₈"   1⁵⁄₈"
MM
1⁵⁄₈"   1⁵⁄₈"
1⁵⁄₈"   1⁵⁄₈"
5" x 5"

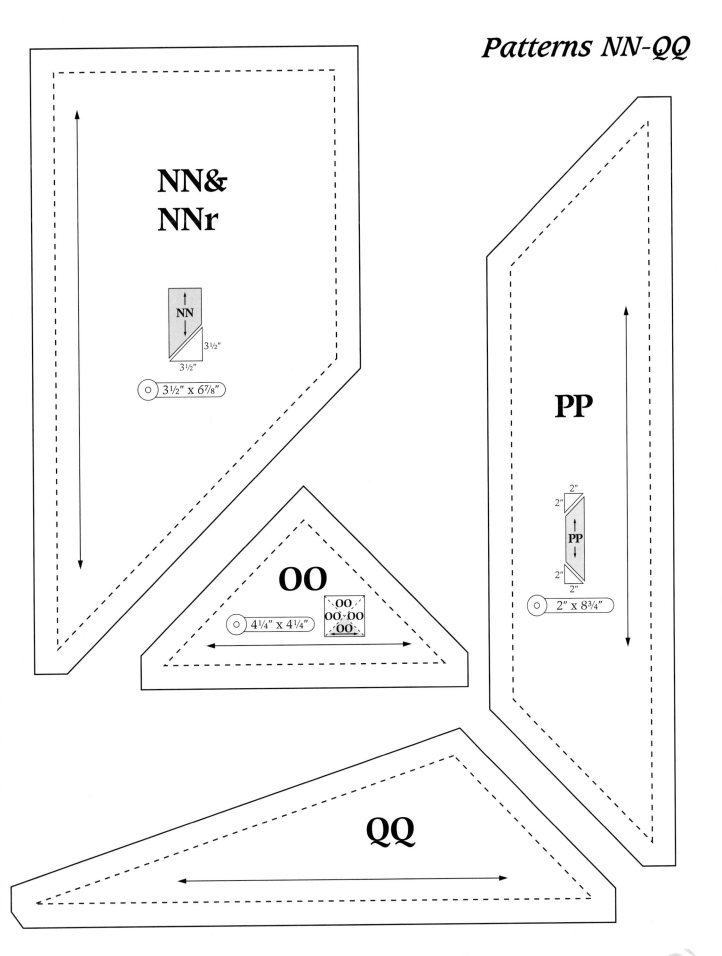

**NN&
NNr**

NN

3½"

3½"

○ 3½" x 6⅞"

OO

4¼" x 4¼"

OO
OO OO
OO

PP

2"

2"

PP

2"

2"

○ 2" x 8¾"

QQ

Patterns RR-VV

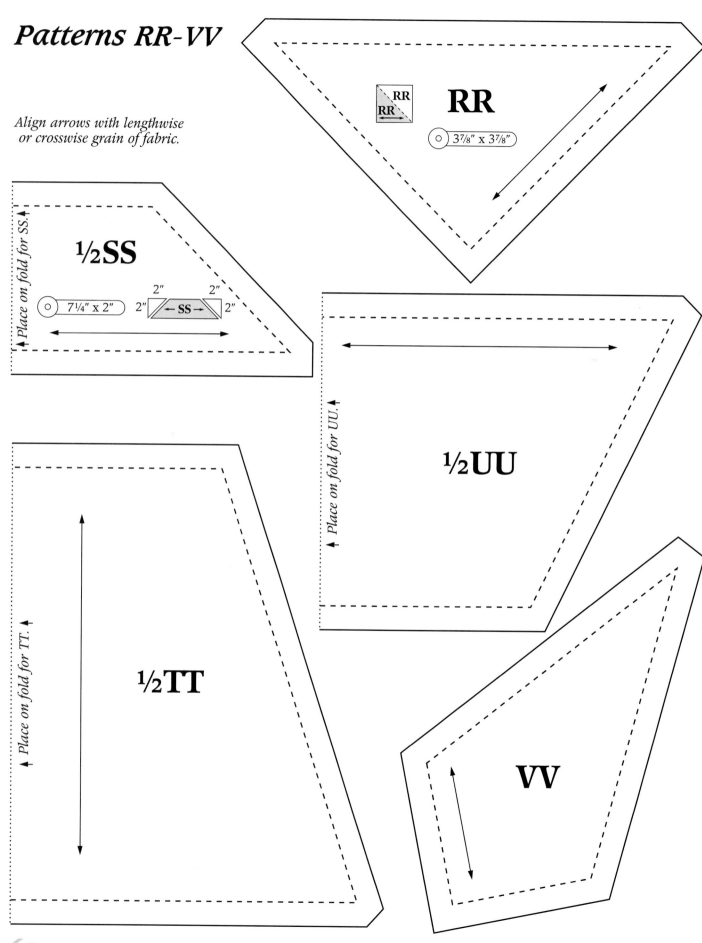

*Align arrows with lengthwise
or crosswise grain of fabric.*

RR

RR
RR

3⁷⁄₈″ x 3⁷⁄₈″

½**SS**

Place on fold for SS.

7¼″ x 2″

2″   2″
2″ ←SS→ 2″

½**UU**

Place on fold for UU.

½**TT**

Place on fold for TT.

VV

General Instructions

This section covers the basic information you will need to make the quilts in this book. It will be especially helpful to beginning quiltmakers, but even those who have sewn quilts for many years may benefit from a quick refresher course. The information is given in the same order as quilts are made, so you will easily be able to find answers to specific questions as they arise. Don't forget that special techniques are explained on pages 4 and 5.

About Sizes

Most of the quilts in this book measure the same size, although some are longer from top to bottom and some are longer from side to side. To help you check your sewing as you proceed, here are the finished (sewn) sizes for all but the three larger quilts.

Design block:
   7½" x 22½"
Borders: 1½" wide
Binding: ⅜" wide
Completed quilt:
   11¼" x 26¼"
plus tabs if desired

Selecting Fabrics

For many quilters, fabric selection is one of the most fun steps of quiltmaking. Of course, you are welcome to try to match the photos to select fabrics that are very close or identical to those used in the original quilts. The fabrics we selected were all readily available at the time we chose them, and none were so special that the quilt could not be made without them. We can also say that there were countless other combinations of fabrics that would have been equally successful.

While selection of fabrics need not be difficult or mysterious, there are a few points that will help.

Skin Tones: We used solid cotton fabrics for most skin tones, but we also chose a tiny check for the New Year baby. Shades range from light pink through various peaches to medium brown. Choose colors that look right to you.

Hair: As with skin tones, you can select hair colors as you wish. The School Kids could have blond hair instead of brown, Cupid could have black hair, and the Leprechaun could have hair in any color of the rainbow (who would know?). We chose prints for hair, mustaches and beards.

Novelty Fabrics: Although cotton fabrics are the traditional choice for quilts, we chose felt for Santa's beard, and you might want to consider other novelty fabrics. When choosing novelty fabrics, look for those that will not stretch and which are about the same weight as cotton. Suggestions include using a man's tie for Dear Old Dad, an antique hankie for the apron on the Pilgrim girl and satin for the angels. If your quilts will ever be washed, of course you will want to choose washable fabrics.

Contrast: To make the figures distinct, it is important that the skin, hair, clothing and other design elements contrast with the background and with each other. When selecting fabrics, stand back several feet and squint to check the contrast. It will also be helpful to collect more than one option (especially since the yardage amounts are small) and

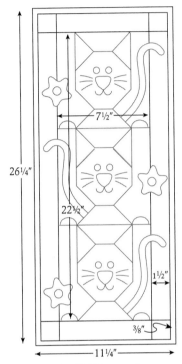

Quilt Dimensions

General Instructions

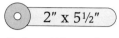

2" x 5½"

Rotary Dimensions

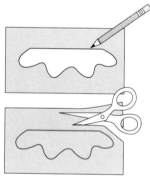

Cutting with scissors

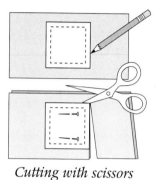

Appliqué Patterns

3-D Patterns

try more than one fabric as you are cutting and sewing.

Prewashing: It is your choice whether or not to wash fabrics before cutting them. Many quilt books offer opinions about the pros and cons of prewashing fabric. It is always a good idea to test fabrics individually to see if the color will run. It's also wise to lightly spray fabric with water and iron it, both to get the folds out of it and to allow fabric to shrink somewhat. Sometimes you will actually see the fabric shrink immediately as it is sprayed!

Cutting Patches

Straight-Edge Patterns: All straight-edged patches can easily be cut with a rotary cutter, and you will find tips for rotary cutting on page 62 with the patterns. Dimensions are given on square and rectangular pattern pieces as well as many patches that are cut from squares and rectangles, so you can simply use those measurements instead of tracing and cutting patterns.

If you prefer, you can cut patches with scissors. To use scissors, you can either mark around

patterns and cut on marked lines, or you can pin the pattern to the fabric and cut around the pattern without marking.

For patches that are reversed (noted with an "r" in the cutting requirements), place pattern face down on fabric before cutting. When you need both a shape and its reverse (such as Q and Qr), place fabric wrong sides together before cutting.

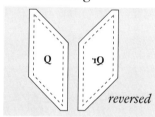

Q   Qr

reversed

Appliqué Patterns: Patterns for appliqué pieces, which are given with the project directions, do not include turn-under allowances. Trace or copy these patterns and cut them out to make templates. Place template face up on right side of fabric and mark around it with a pencil. Add ³⁄₁₆" turn-under allowance (outside the marked lines) when cutting fabrics, judging this distance by eye. Appliqué patches are cut with scissors instead of with a rotary cutter.

3-D Appliqué: For 3-D appliqué patches, mark one pattern shape on the wrong side of fabric. Then place another layer of fabric (right sides touching) under the marked fabric and cut both layers at one time. Leave these pairs of patches together so they are ready for sewing.

Piecing

Machine piecing is perfect for these quilts. Use neutral-color thread (such as a medium beige or gray) if you prefer not to change thread colors for various fabrics.

As for all machine piecing, there are two important points to keep in mind. First, be sure your seam allowances are an accurate ¼" width to assure that all pieces will fit well.

Use ¼" seams

Tape as a guide

Second, whenever a patch has an angled or "set-in" seam such as the example shown, begin or end the line of sewing exactly at the seam line, not at the edge of the patch. The seam that forms the adjacent part of the angle will begin at exactly the same point. Find more information about set-in seams on page 30.

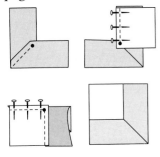

Set-in Patches

Appliqué

Appliqué patches are sewn after the piecing is finished, except in the case of patches that are partially included in a seam. One example is the paws on the cats. Because the straight edges are enclosed in the block seams, the paws should be appliquéd before joining blocks. Project directions will guide you in the best order for sewing.

Hand Appliqué: To do hand appliqué, place the marked and cut patch face up on the quilt top. Baste it in place or use one or two pins to hold it. Use a single strand of thread that matches the appliqué (not the background); tie a small knot

in the end of the thread. Turn under the allowance with the point of the needle and sew just inside the marked line with a blind stitch.

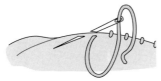

Blind Stitch

Stitches should be about ⅛" apart and most likely will not show.

Clip turn-under allowances on inside (concave) curves.

Clip inside curves

End the line of sewing with a couple of small backstitches. Trim away the background behind the appliqué if it will show through.

Machine Appliqué: This technique uses invisible nylon thread and a blind-hem stitch. Prepare patches by turning under allowances and basting them, then pin or baste them in place on the quilt top. Set the machine for a short stitch length and narrow width and sew a blind-hem stitch around the patch.

Embroidery

Many of the quilts use simple embroidery for details. Although colors are specified in project directions, you can certainly choose any colors you like. Also, you can choose either cotton embroidery floss or no. 8 pearl cotton. Use two or three ply of floss or a single strand of size 8 pearl cotton. Silk embroidery floss and novelty threads offer additional choices. Select a needle with an eye just large enough to thread the needle. A crewel needle or sharp, size 5 to 10, would be a good choice. A small embroidery hoop might be helpful but is not necessary.

Project directions include a tracing pattern for embroidered details. The center of the patch (especially for faces) or other placement guides are given to help you position the design. Fold the patch to find the center and place it over the tracing pattern, matching centers. Use a pencil to lightly mark the design. When beginning to embroider, leave a tail about ½" long on the back side and catch it with the stitches. When ending, weave the threaded needle back through on the wrong

Machine appliqué with blind-hem stitch

Embroidery Tracing Guide

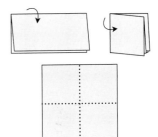

Folding to find center

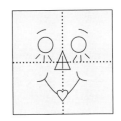

Align centers & trace

Weave in ends

General Instructions

Outline Stitch

Backstitch

Straight Stitch

Chain Stitch

Satin Stitch

Lazy Daisy Stitch

Buttonhole Stitch

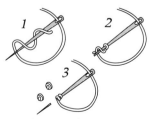
French Knots

side. Trim tails carefully so they don't show.

Stitches: Suggested stitches are specified in project directions. However, you can substitute similar stitches to achieve the same effect.

For straight or curved lines: use either outline stitch or backstitch.

For short, straight lines: use a single straight stitch.

For wider lines: use one or two rows of chain stitch.

For solid areas: use satin stitch.

For petals: use lazy daisy stitches.

For eyelashes: use buttonhole stitch.

For eyes and other small details: use one or more french knots.

Adding Borders & Corner Squares

All of the small quilts in this book have long borders (K), short borders (F) and corner squares (A). After completing the quilt design block, you will be ready to add borders and corner squares. Border dimensions for larger quilts are given with project directions.

Sew long borders to long edges of quilt top. Press seam allowances

toward borders. Sew corner squares to ends of short borders. Press seam allowances toward short borders. Sew a short border/corner square to one short edge of the quilt top; repeat for the other short edge. Press the seam allowances toward the borders.

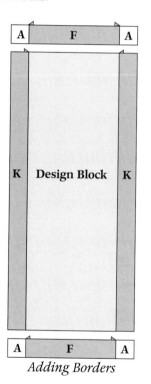
Adding Borders

Assembling the Layers & Quilting

Check the quilt top to be sure that dark threads or seam allowances do not show through. If necessary, give the quilt top a final pressing.

Cut the lining as called for in the project directions, and iron it to eliminate creases or wrinkles. Spread lining on a table; tape it in place (optional).

Cut the batting to be the same size as the lining and lay it on top of the lining. Smooth any wrinkles.

Center the quilt top over the batting. Use straight pins to hold the layers together. Baste the layers together, either with running stitches (about 1″ to 2″ long) or hold the layers together with small safety pins. Avoid basting along seams or areas that will be quilted. You will find

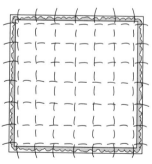

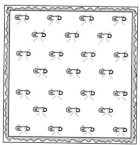
Basting Quilts

quilting diagrams with the project directions. Also baste ⅛" from all edges of the quilt top. This basting should remain after the quilting is finished to make it easier to do the binding.

Quilting: Working either by hand or by machine, quilt in-the-ditch as shown in the quilting diagram. To quilt in-the-ditch, sew along the seam line on the "low" side of the seam, which is the side without the seam allowances.

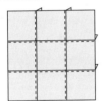

In-the-Ditch Quilting

Quilting in-the-ditch around appliqués will make those patches puff up a bit. Add other quilting as you wish.

Adding Tabs or a Sleeve

To prepare the quilt for adding optional ribbon or fabric tabs or a sleeve

and binding, trim lining and batting to extend beyond the quilt top by ⅛". This will give you a finished binding width of ⅜".

For ribbon tabs, select ribbon in any width and cut pieces 5" long. You will need 4 pieces for the vertical quilts, and 5 or 6 pieces for the horizontal quilts. These tabs are added after the binding is finished. Fold each piece in half and position them on the back of the quilt so they extend 1¾" above the binding. Pin in place. Tack in place by hand, or machine sew from the front of the quilt (in-the-ditch) next to the binding.

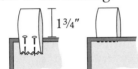

Ribbon Tabs

For narrow tabs that will finish 1½" wide, cut 8 D patches in the fabric of your choice. If you need to purchase fabric, ⅛ yard will be plenty.

For wide tabs that will finish 4½" wide, cut 8 S patches. If you need to purchase fabric, ¼ yard is the amount to get.

Prepare fabric tabs by sewing two tab patches,

right sides together, along opposite sides. Sew with a ¼" seam and turn right side out. Press flat. Repeat to make four tabs (or more for a larger quilt).

Fold tabs in half so the raw edges match. Working on the back side of the quilt, position and pin four tabs evenly spaced across the upper edge of the quilt. The outer two tabs should be ⅜" from the edges of the lining. The binding will be sewn over the raw edges of the tabs.

A sleeve is a tube of fabric sewn to the back side of the quilt (at the top) to accommodate a rod for hanging. To make a sleeve, cut a piece of lining fabric 6" wide and 1" longer than the quilt width. Hem both short ends by folding over ½" and another ½" and sewing. With wrong sides together, match long edges. Baste sleeve to back of quilt so that raw edges will be covered with binding. After the binding is finished, blind stitch the lower edge of the sleeve to the quilt lining.

Binding the Quilt

If you have not added tabs or a sleeve, be sure

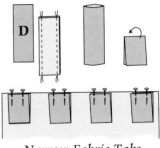

Narrow Fabric Tabs

Wide Fabric Tabs

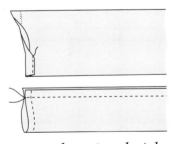

Hem sleeve & make tube

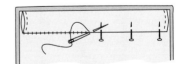

Blindstitch sleeve to the quilt

General Instructions

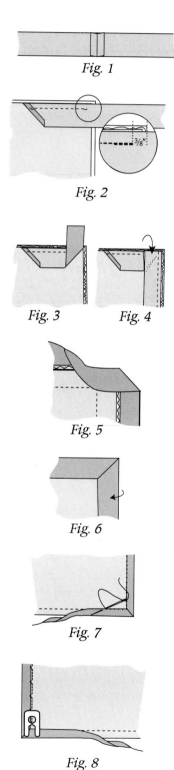

Fig. 1

Fig. 2

Fig. 3   *Fig. 4*

Fig. 5

Fig. 6

Fig. 7

Fig. 8

to trim lining and batting to extend beyond the quilt top by ⅛". This will allow a finished binding width of ⅜".

The instructions for each small quilt project call for binding 1½" x 83". (Requirements for each larger quilt are given with project directions.) Depending on the width of your fabric, you will need to cut either two or three 1½"-wide strips across the width of the fabric. Join strips end-to-end; press seam allowances open. (Fig. 1)

Binding is sewn in either of two ways. You can sew it to the front of the quilt (through all layers) and then turn it to the back and sew it by hand. If you prefer, you can sew the binding to the back of the quilt (through all layers) and then turn it to the front and sew it by machine. We will tell you how to work both ways.

Fold the end of the binding strip in a 45° angle; press. Trim strip to leave ¼" seam allowance. Working on a table and starting on one long side of quilt (not at a corner), pin right side of binding to quilt (either the front side or the back side). Be careful not to stretch the edge of the quilt.

Machine stitch (through all layers) ⅜" from edge of the lining (or ¼" from the edge of the quilt top), stopping the line of sewing ⅜" from the next edge of the lining. Backstitch; cut threads. (Fig. 2)

Lay the quilt flat on a table. Fold the binding strip away from the quilt (Fig. 3), then fold it down again to position the binding strip along the next edge of the quilt. (Fig. 4) Pin binding in place. Stitch from the fold of the binding along this edge, again stopping ⅜" from next edge. Repeat this procedure until the binding has been sewn all around the quilt. Overlap ends and cut off any excess binding.

Turn binding to other side of the quilt and fold under the ⅜" seam allowance. Pin the folded edge in place, just covering the first line of sewing. At each corner, fold binding in the sequence shown to make a miter. (Figs. 5 and 6)

Sew the folded edge in place by either of two methods. Working on the back side of the quilt, you can use hand-sewn blind stitching and thread to match the binding. (Fig. 7) Catch just the lining or the lin-

ing and the tabs or sleeve, but do not sew through the quilt top.

If you prefer, you can use machine blind stitching on the front of the quilt that just catches the edge of the binding. Use invisible thread (on top) and thread to match the binding (in the bobbin), and sew on the front side of the quilt. (Fig. 8) This sewing will go through all layers and can also catch the tabs to hold them extending up and away from the quilt.

Adding a Label

It's always a nice touch to make and add a label. One easy way to do this is to enlarge the drawing of your quilt (see the coloring pages) and trace it on muslin with a Pigma permanent pen. Sign your name, the name of the quilt, and the date, then appliqué the label to the quilt lining with blind stitch.

*Happy Quilter
Star-Spangled Cats
July 4, 1996*

Quilt Label

About the Authors

Marie Shirer *"I had a great time making some of the quilts for this book. Sewing the Raggedy Ann and Raggedy Andy quilts brought back special memories of my childhood. It was fun playing with dolls again!"* Marie, also the coauthor of *Christmas on Parade*, has written seven quilting books. A lifelong quiltmaker, she joined the Leman Publications family as an editor for *Quilter's Newsletter Magazine* in 1982 after owning a quilt and needlework store in Kansas for several years.

Marla Stefanelli *"My biggest goal in creating the patterns for this book was to make sure that they would be simple to sew for quilters of all skill levels–that's important to me!"* Marla made her first quilt 20 years ago and hasn't stopped since! She has been a member of the Leman Publications team since 1982, designing quilt patterns for *Quilter's Newsletter Magazine*, *Quiltmaker* and *Quilts & Other Comforts*. She is also the coauthor of *Christmas on Parade*.

Cynthia Harmer *"I come from a family that believed learning to sew, crochet, knit and embroider was a part of growing up!"* Cynthia joined the Leman staff just in time to assist with the designs and illustrations for both this book and *Christmas on Parade*. Before then she owned a successful graphic-design business and an art-to-wear clothing business. Her fiber art has won several awards over the years.

Clockwise starting at left: Marie Shirer, Marla Stefanelli and Cynthia Harmer.

Coloring Pages

Use the drawings on these two pages to play with colors. We suggest that you take this page to a copy center and have the drawings enlarged at least 200%. Then use felt markers, colored pencils or crayons to try out various color combinations. You can also use enlargements of these drawings to make quilt labels, gift tags and greeting cards. Invite children to join in the fun!